ADDITIONAL PRAISE FOR
DR. JIM AFREMOW AND
THE CHAMPION'S COMEBACK

"*The Champion's Comeback* will take your mind-set to the next level. If there is one thing I learned over my 17-year track and field career, it is that the mind is what will always make the difference. This book is packed with knowledge for any athlete, coach, or entrepreneur who is wanting to step their mind-set up to the next level."

—IAN WARNER, 2012 Olympian and
owner of BounceBackEntrepreneurs.com

"At some point, and likely right NOW, all of us are in need of a comeback. But how do we get started? And where can we get help? *The Champion's Comeback* by Jim Afremow is your playbook. Using stories and strategies from the greats, Jim simplifies the steps to get started, adjust your mind-set, form beliefs, overcome setbacks, and ultimately achieve your Champion's Comeback. Definitely a recommended read."

—JOE JACOBI, Olympic gold medalist and
chief executive officer for USA Canoe/Kayak

"*The Champion's Comeback* is a must-read for any athlete striving to achieve. Jim deals with pressure and the fear of failure head on. His well-written and simple advice is accompanied by extensive tangible examples to maximize performance when under pressure. This is applicable for all ages, abilities, and situations for the athlete, coach, or even those in the business world."

—DICK GOULD, director of tennis, Stanford University,
coach of 17 NCAA Championship teams

"The power of positivity and the right mental approach is crucial in any sports field and in life in general. Dr. Afremow's book *The Champion's Comeback* can help lead you in the right direction."

—BEN HENDERSON, mixed martial artist and
former UFC lightweight champion

"*The Champion's Comeback* has not only inspired us to re-frame our retirement from professional sports but also has empowered us to inspire the next generation of elite athletes through the daily rigors of competitive sports."

—LAUREN AND RYAN MARIANO, RPM Sand Volleyball

PRAISE FOR
THE CHAMPION'S MIND

"Athletes who want to learn the secrets of the mental game should read *The Champion's Mind*."

—CARLI LLOYD, two-time Olympic gold medalist, 2014 FIFA Women's World Cup Champion, and 2015 FIFA World Player of the Year

"*The Champion's Mind* is a mental training book that will help you reach your potential in sports. I highly recommend this book to all athletes and coaches."

—JACKIE SLATER, NFL Hall of Famer

"*The Champion's Mind* reveals the mental skills and strategies Olympic champions use to perform their best when it matters most. Dr. Afremow's matchless book is a must for athletes and coaches."

—SHANNON MILLER, Olympic gold medalist in gymnastics and president of Shannon Miller Lifestyle

"How sweet it is to breathe that rarefied air of a high-performance athlete! How refreshing it is, as well, to recognize so many of the techniques in Dr. Afremow's book that get you to that privileged place. *The Champion's Mind* is a simple, straightforward elixir for the high achiever in all of us."

—MORTEN ANDERSEN, NFL's all-time leading scorer and a member of the NFL's All-Decade Teams for the 1980s and 1990s

"I read this book with my eyes wide open, and the content continued to keep them open at all times. Jim's advice and tips are very simple and easy to understand. Read only one chapter at a time and apply it to your approach to tennis, sports, and life."

—NICK BOLLETTIERI, founder and president of Nick Bollettieri IMG Tennis Academy

"Athletes can unlock a new level of performance by learning the power of training their mind as they train their body. From preparation to rehabilitation to competition, *The Champion's Mind* gives the mental guidance necessary to allow an athlete to reach their full athletic potential. Dr. Afremow's playbook for increasing mental strength gives clear direction to make the reader a better athlete, a better teammate, and a better person."

—CURT TOMASEVICZ, Olympic gold medalist in four-man bobsled

"*The Champion's Mind* is loaded with great lessons, advice, and perspectives on how to be successful. It is definitely not a requirement to be an athlete or a coach in order to benefit from this book. The skills and strategies that Jim provides here are essential in carving a path to success, no matter what field you are in or what your goals are. I can honestly say that I have lived by many of the strategies offered in this book, and I can also say I wish I had lived by more of them. But it's never too late to be as good as you can be!"

—DAN JANSEN, Olympic gold medalist in speed skating
and former world record holder

"What tends to differentiate the all-stars from the rest of the pack resides between the ears. Jim Afremow does a great job exploring this subject in *The Champion's Mind*. This is a great book for coaches and athletes of all ages who are looking to improve performance at any level, in any sport."

—SHAWN GREEN, two-time MLB All-Star

"Dr. Afremow nails all the basics and gives readers an excellent window into how a champion's mind works before and during 'the process.'"

—RANDY CROSS, three-time Super Bowl champion

"One can always learn from others. *The Champion's Mind* holds a wealth of insight as to how you can become a winner in your everyday life."

—PHIL MAHRE, Olympic gold medalist in alpine skiing

"It's amazing to see how Dr. Afremow points out what athletes go through every day. He describes a lot of situations that I have experienced as well. In this book, you can find a lot of simple but very useful tips and principles that might help you improve your performance."

—BRITTA HEIDEMANN, three-time Olympian in épée fencing
and gold medalist at the 2008 Beijing Olympics

"*The Champion's Mind* is very informative and full of great principles and guidelines for any athlete who is searching for excellence in their performance."

—MIKE CANDREA, Olympic gold medal coach of the US softball team
and eight-time national champion coach of the University of Arizona
women's softball team

"Dr. Afremow hits a grand slam with *The Champion's Mind*. Every athlete should keep a copy of this book in their locker or gym bag."

—LEAH O'BRIEN-AMICO, three-time Olympic gold medalist
for the US softball team

"We all have an athlete in us; we were all born to run, jump, swim, and compete in some way or another. The gold medal at an Olympic Games has been declared as the highest honor to reward discipline, commitment, power, strength, finesse, passion, precision, patience, speed, and skill, just to name a few. You too can go for gold in all areas of your life by following Jim's strategies. Decide what you want and go after it with all you have to give, every single day. Daily acts of excellence are the secret. Choose your success today."

—*NATALIE COOK,* five-time Olympian in beach volleyball
and gold medalist at the 2000 Sydney Olympics

"Do you want to learn how the best in the world got there? In *The Champion's Mind,* Jim distills a myriad of golden Olympic stories into clear tools we all can use. I am positive that you will read insights in this book that will help you rise to the top of your discipline. If you read this book, you will be inspired. Thank you, Jim, for writing this book!"

—*ADAM KREEK,* two-time Olympian in men's eight rowing
and gold medalist at the 2008 Beijing Olympics

"When I read *The Champion's Mind*, it quite frankly reminded me of many instances, mannerisms, and thoughts leading to my Olympic championship, and it has given me many other wisdoms to pass on to the athletes I now coach. Choose your path, follow your path; any path worth choosing will have its ups and downs, but *The Champion's Mind* will help you with ideas to keep moving forward on that path. The focus you gain will help you reach the top of whatever you seek."

—*NICK HYSONG,* Olympic gold medalist in the pole vault

"Dr. Afremow's training and tips have been an important part of the preparation and success of our athletes when they take the Wonderlic test at the NFL combine. In *The Champion's Mind*, Dr. Afremow provides simple yet powerfully effective strategies to help athletes and coaches reach their full potential."

—*MARK VERSTEGEN,* founder and president of
Athletes' Performance and Core Performance

THE
CHAMPION'S
COMEBACK

THE
CHAMPION'S
COMEBACK

HOW GREAT ATHLETES
RECOVER, REFLECT,
AND
REIGNITE

JIM AFREMOW, PhD

RODALE.

RODALE *wellness*

Live happy. Be healthy. Get inspired.

Sign up today to get exclusive access to our authors, exclusive bonuses,
and the most authoritative, useful, and cutting edge information on health,
wellness, fitness, and living your life to the fullest.

Visit us online at RodaleWellness.com
Join us at RodaleWellness.com/Join

Rodale books may be purchased for business or promotional use or for special sales.
For information, please write to:
Special Markets Department, Rodale Inc., 733 Third Avenue, New York, NY 10017.

Printed in the United States of America

Rodale Inc. makes every effort to use acid-free ♾, recycled paper ♾.

Book design by Amy C. King

Library of Congress Cataloging-in-Publication Data is on file with the publisher.
ISBN-13: 978-1-62336-679-7

Distributed to the trade by Macmillan
2 4 6 8 10 9 7 5 3 1 hardcover

We inspire and enable people to improve their lives and the world around them.
rodalebooks.com

To my wife, Anne,
and our daughter, Maria Paz

I have one thing to say
to those nonbelievers:
Don't ever underestimate
the heart of a champion!

—RUDY TOMJANOVICH,
coach of the 1994 and 1995 NBA champions Houston Rockets

CONTENTS

INTRODUCTION
COMING BACK IN SPORTS
AND IN LIFE

Your setback is the platform for your comeback.

—ANONYMOUS

Grasping the baton from the hand of *The Champion's Mind: How Great Athletes Think, Train, and Thrive*, this book looks at how all great champions continue to persevere despite losses, injuries, and other personal and professional setbacks. Success in sports rarely follows a straight line or predictable path.

The Champion's Comeback zeros in on how champions learn to repeat their successes and pick themselves up after setbacks by consistently practicing positive habits and thought patterns. This book is for people of all ages and all levels of competition. If you have the heart and desire to get back in your game and compete like a champion, this book is for you.

Here's how I've chosen to organize this book. Chapter One discusses what I call the Champion's Comeback Code. We will learn the 7 L's, strategies champions use to bounce back from common athletic setbacks—whether mistakes, lopsided scores, or crushing disappointments—and come back stronger.

Chapter Two examines a few remarkable sports comebacks and the lessons we can all learn from them. In doing so, we'll see that setbacks show a champion's true colors. We'll see how champions turn adversity into an advantage. Above all else, we'll see that champions take pride in comebacks, relishing the opportunity to come back stronger. They don't dwell on what they've lost. Rather, they learn from losses and focus on what they stand to gain, propelling themselves forward with positivity.

Chapter Three provides colorful examples of comebacks in team sports. We'll see the 7 L's in action and find inspiration to help us put them to work in our own game and life. We'll learn powerful team concepts for how to practice and play like a champion, as well as the importance of developing healthy relationships in sports and life to achieve personal excellence and peak athletic performance.

Chapter Four brings to light how the right state of mind can be the difference between winning and losing—it can turn a talented athlete into one of the best to ever play, no matter the sport. We'll learn practical tools and techniques to bounce back from common mental game problems such as motivational lags, inner doubts, and performance jitters.

Chapter Five explores challenges that are specific to fitness participants and endurance athletes. We'll learn techniques for overcoming "gymtimidation" and braving new fitness challenges as well as how to cope with the commonplace postperformance blues. We'll also learn about the psychology of commitment and how champions dig deeper, move past physical discomforts, and go the distance.

Chapter Six examines how Michael Jordan, a champion's champion, overcame setbacks and naysayers to reach the summit of the Mount Olympus of basketball greatness. In particular, we'll see how the 7 L's are revealed in Jordan's Hall of Fame induction speech. We can all draw inspiration from Jordan's example to keep driving toward success to become a champion in our chosen sport.

Chapter Seven offers eight detailed scripts to guide you through powerful visualizations. These scripts will help you visualize success, whether for the first time or after a setback. They include visualizations for comebacks, running marathons, achieving fitness goals, and recovering from injury. Visualization, if consistently practiced, builds a tight bridge between the mental and the physical. You'll be able to see the victory and then achieve it.

Chapter Eight observes how Michigan State University men's basketball head coach Tom Izzo, golf legend Ben Hogan, and tennis star Serena Williams reached the pinnacle of their professions, made remarkable comebacks, and refused to back down even when victory seemed out of reach. Like these great champions, readers will learn how to hang tough in the face of the impossible and transform minor setbacks into major comebacks.

Sports comebacks come in all shapes and sizes: Athletes come back from devastating injuries, underdogs overcome seemingly insurmountable deficits just before the clock strikes zero, home teams bounce back from tough losses to redeem themselves against crosstown rivals, and former stars come out of retirement to show they've still got it.

Each one of the *sports* comebacks we'll discuss can teach us about overcoming similar *life* problems: health issues, job loss, issues at the office, educational challenges such as learning disabilities, or any personal loss.

Setbacks are your opportunity to bounce back—to make a comeback!

CHAPTER ONE

CRACKING THE COMEBACK CODE

I can choose either to be a victim of the world
or an adventurer in search of treasure.
It's all a question of how I view my life.

—PAULO COELHO, NOVELIST

Two kinds of players show up in sports and life: the *contender* and the *champion*.

The contender, threatened by the prospect of competition and failure, either refuses help or expects others to do the hard work he should be doing himself. You can picture the contender's attitude like a downward-pointing triangle.

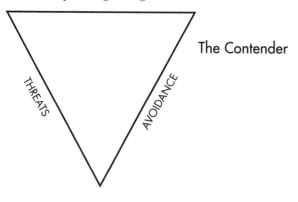

The Contender

THREATS

AVOIDANCE

In contrast, the champion seeks out tough challenges and opportunities to learn and grow and looks for support and feedback from teammates, coaches, and others. Picture this perspective like an upward-pointing triangle.

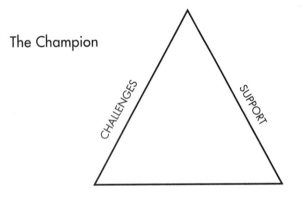

The Champion

CHALLENGES

SUPPORT

A champion, unlike a contender, regroups after inevitable setbacks and emerges stronger. A champion embraces difficult and demanding situations and learns from both triumph and failure.

"Life is not a spectator sport," said baseball legend Jackie Robinson. "If you're going to spend your whole life in the grandstand just watching what goes on, in my opinion you're wasting your life." In other words, to make the journey more worthwhile, life should be viewed as a participatory sport—*play life!*

Everyone can, and should, come down from the grandstand and embrace challenges on the field of play. That's how we move from being spectators to being contenders. Once taking on challenges becomes a habit, you truly become a champion. Participate, participate, and participate in your sport—no matter the challenges or obstacles ahead.

The ability to step up to challenges is important in all aspects of life, and it's a key ingredient of happiness and success. Challenges will appear in all sorts of situations, from trying out for a team to working on a new move or skill (and putting it into action during a game or scrimmage) to pitting yourself against stronger competition or trying a new fitness activity. These situations will likely involve emotional and physical discomforts and the risk of failure and rejection, but these are all part of the process of becoming a champion.

Consider this story: The day after graduating from high school, Vanessa paused in front of a storefront she had breezed past so many times before. This time, on a whim, Vanessa opened the door and walked right under the beat-up EXPERT PSYCHIC READINGS sign. A gentle middle-aged woman greeted her before giving her a not-so-gentle reading: "You have a most miserable future." Vanessa was determined to escape her fate. She tried to defy the prediction by being extremely cautious, never taking risks, and steering away from anything that might cause her harm. At the ripe old age of 100, Vanessa took her last breath and realized—too late—that the fortune-teller's prediction had come true. She had led an empty, miserable life.

It may seem counterintuitive, but failure is the greatest teacher. We learn best by making mistakes or experiencing disappointments. If you allow the fear of failure to prevail, then you've already ensured your own failure by depriving yourself of life's greatest teacher. As all-time hockey great Wayne Gretzky said, "You miss 100 percent of the shots you don't take."

In sports, in particular, athletes receive instant feedback on their performance, what works and what doesn't—and that's a great thing! It means they've just learned something new about their game and have the opportunity to improve. Weaknesses can always be turned into strengths.

Do you give up after just one loss or a tough race, game, or meet? It's important to realize that all champions have lost and made mistakes—more than you can count! Psychiatrist Milton Erickson said, "Along with successes, collect a proper number of failures." Collecting failures in sports is how you retool and return to competition as a superior athlete. Look at it this way: Failures can be a source of motivation, not discouragement.

You must, however, make adjustments, big and small. Think of the Jewish proverb "I ask not for a lighter burden, but for broader shoulders." The contender yearns to lighten the load, while the champion wants the ability to take on more. This is a crucial distinction, because we can't always control the demands placed on us; all we can do is have the mental fortitude to respond. Starting now, instead of cursing daily difficulties, ask yourself, "How can I best carry my load?"

This adjustment requires you to redefine difficulties as challenges. Contenders feel threatened by playing against stiff competition or trying new fitness challenges. They are worried about falling behind or receiving negative evaluations or criticism from others and are intimidated by the prospect of physical discomfort.

Contenders don't seem to have much fun playing. They either complain about everything or deny having any issues ("I'm good!") and distract themselves to escape their problems. If they try to deal with everything on their own, it will take them longer to achieve their goals, assuming they can do that at all.

Unlike contenders, champions thrive on embracing challenges because these challenges push them and make them feel most alive, improve their competitiveness as athletes, and allow them to mature as individuals. In fact, champions see everything as a trial that tests and improves them.

This point is critical: How you think about an upcoming performance and what will happen to you (facing a challenge, losing a point, making a mistake) will significantly influence your feelings and actions. If you view an upcoming situation as a threat, then you will panic and perform poorly. You might even completely avoid the situation.

By the same token, if you view the upcoming performance as a challenge, then you can get excited. By overcoming your initial fears and gaining confidence, you will be highly motivated and have the freedom to perform your best and you will focus only on the things you can control. At this point and in this frame of mind, you will take on challenges like a champion.

"There's always going to be adversity, there's always going to be challenges, and those are all opportunities to rise above," said Kobe Bryant, a five-time NBA champion with the Los Angeles Lakers. What he is implying is that after a setback, contenders collapse while champions rise.

Comebacks can be small, such as recovering from an error or a penalty in a game, or large, such as returning to a sport after a major injury or a long absence. For a champion, there is nothing more magnificent or memorable than making a major comeback. The bigger the setback, the more opportunities to learn and the more glory and satisfaction to be gained upon a successful comeback.

A champion must respond to some, and possibly all, of these 12 common athletic setbacks.

1. A mistake or an error

2. Being down in a game (or race, fight, match, series)

3. One or more shattering defeats

4. Crushing disappointment

5. A close call or a near victory

6. Being benched

7. A performance slump

8. The low (or high) expectations of others

9. An injury or an illness

10. An extended absence

11. Feeling pressure to continue winning

12. A fitness slump

How will you achieve your goal and how can you adapt and respond to various challenges? Going through setbacks in sports and other areas of life is perfectly normal, as nobody can avoid such things. How you choose to deal with setbacks—such as threats or challenges—is what makes the difference. "One can choose to go back toward safety or forward toward growth," wrote psychologist Abraham Maslow. "Growth must be chosen again and again; fear must be overcome again and again."

We all want to make thinking, feeling, and acting like a champion part of our everyday life because, let's face it, demands and difficulties are part of all aspects of life. Making the move from contender to champion means stepping out of your comfort zone, calling on your inner strength and supporters, and reframing tough situations as growth opportunities and chances for comebacks.

Getting to the top requires hard work, good luck, and positive support. However, a comeback adds the potential of failure, injury, fear, and criticism. Which sounds harder? A comeback, of course.

Here are the 7 L's that champions use to crack the Champion's Comeback Code.

1. **LET GO**—release the mental brick

2. **LOOK FOR SUPPORT**—build a winning team

3. **LOVE THE GAME**—compete with purpose and passion

4. **LEARN**—embrace a growth mind-set

5. **LABOR**—keep pounding the rock

6. **LEARN OPTIMISM**—believe in your comeback story

7. **LEAN ON YOUR MENTAL GAME**—win the game from within yourself

LET GO:
RELEASE THE MENTAL BRICK

*Renew, release, let go. Yesterday's gone.
There's nothing you can do to bring it back. You can't "should've"
done something. You can only do something. Renew yourself.
Release that attachment. Today is a new day!*

—STEVE MARABOLI, AUTHOR AND SPEAKER

We are not machines, we're humans made of bones, skin, and emotions. For almost all of life's important moments, you will follow routines or rituals, though they may differ from society to society and person to person. We perform them because they help us control our emotions, forge our ties with others, and move on to the next challenge.

Why does Rafael Nadal dominate the French Open? Sure, he pounds the ball with tremendous topspin during his matches and chases down every ball until his opponent collapses, but what is he thinking? A champion's thoughts. Just watch while the "King of Clay" sits and takes a break and you'll see him going through his mental and physical routines: Nadal takes two sips from two bottles, one with water, the other with an electrolyte mixture. He puts both bottles back in the same spot every time. With a towel on his lap, he breathes deeply. Racket in hand, he checks his strings.

Similarly, notice what LeBron James does during time-outs. What is the four-time NBA Most Valuable Player doing and where is his mind when he isn't running up and down the court making baskets? Note the mechanics of his break routine. He is supremely focused—not on yelling at fans or joking around but on simply *stopping and resting*. He takes a true break: Lebron takes two of sips of water, sits calmly, closes his eyes, and practices slow and deep breathing.

Rafael Nadal's and LeBron James's respective routines—their "habits of champions"—keep them focused, help them relax, and recharge the muscle that works the hardest in sports and in life: the brain.

So what's your routine?

Following a mistake by your team or a good play by the opposition, think "Drop it" or "Park it" and move on. Have a go-to phrase to release and quickly refocus on the purpose at hand. For instance, volleyball players can clap their hands and say "Next ball" after a missed shot or "Keep swinging" after getting a shot blocked.

After suffering a loss, how do champions move forward on a positive track instead of tracking the negative? Following any kind of setback, champions tell themselves and their teammates to have a "short memory." A short memory is the best medication for managing mistakes and losses throughout a long season. The next game provides a brand-new occasion to play like a champion.

After a setback or a failure, especially a devastating one, it can be important to implement a ritual that helps you turn the page. For example, after a shattering defeat, a team can dig a hole in the ground at their next practice and bury a game ball as a symbolic gesture to let go of that loss and look forward to the next game.

Leaving your game behind at the pitch, court, or rink is important. For self-care, especially after a difficult day, take a shower at night and wash everything away. Think, "I did what I could today," "I'm washing away what I saw and heard today," and "Today is done and now I'm ready for the next day." This physical and mental cleansing will give you a positive attitude and a renewed spirit.

LOOK FOR SUPPORT: BUILD A WINNING TEAM

Life is not a solo act. It's a huge collaboration, and we all need to assemble around us the people who care about us and support us in times of strife.

—TIM GUNN, ACTOR

When young athletes are developing, they are like sponges, quickly absorbing everything around them. More mature athletes are more like machines: Parts are locked in place, movements are grooved in, and skill sets are becoming dependable resources.

So what happens after a devastating loss, injury, or decline that challenges all prior approaches? Is it possible to adjust something by yourself that for years had worked well but now doesn't work anymore? Can you depend on old habits when facing new circumstances? Is the best approach to "do the same thing over and over again and yet expect different results?" This is the time to turn to a specialist, such as a mental coach, and learn new ways of doing old things.

Achieving your goals requires committed support along the way. To be a champion, take the initiative to speak to experts, such as sports coaches and sports psychologists, for specific guidance and reach out to family and friends for support. You will likely gain good information and feel better as a result.

For example, the modern game of tennis requires pros to travel with an entourage of fitness trainers, mental coaches, nutritionists, and others. Similarly, NFL teams have a comprehensive sports medicine team, IT staff, and many other employees. We too often just think a player is great on his or her own merit, but that's because the media pays very little attention to the support staff.

As far as your own "entourage" is concerned, make sure to surround yourself with positive people. To do this, take whatever steps are necessary to bring your support in closer. Limit contacts with people who drain your energy or distract you from your dreams. Remember, true friends and teammates *lift you up*. Be mindful but wary of the critics. In other words, don't drink the "hater-ade" that will likely be all around you.

Basketball player Christian Laettner is a prime example of how a champion faced a turning of the tide and used that energy to become even better. He led the Duke Blue Devils to back-to-back

NCAA Championships, in 1991 and 1992, making several clutch shots—most famously, the buzzer beater to knock Kentucky out of the 1992 NCAA tournament. Laettner then played on the Dream Team that won gold in a dominant fashion at the 1992 Olympics. He retired after 13 seasons in the NBA, which included an all-star selection in 1997.

The ESPN *30 for 30* documentary "I Hate Christian Laettner" examines how the 6'11" center from Angola, New York, became the supervillain of college hoops. Duke fans loved him, but others loved to hate him. In March 2015, while promoting the documentary as a guest on ESPN's *Mike & Mike Show*, Laettner was asked whether he relished the fact that he was so hated. He said he tried to use the criticism to his advantage.

> Well, I don't relish it, and you don't set out in life trying to have people hate you or dislike you. But there's only so much you can do with it. And you're not going to lose sleep over it, and you're not going to cry over it. So you've got to try to use it and spin it to your advantage in some way if you can. So I tried to let it fuel me and motivate me to play harder and play better, and that's really all you can do with it. Because if you don't spin it and use it that way, then you're going to lose sleep over it.

It is sometimes vital to build a mental buffer against naysayers. It is particularly important during a comeback when we can be more vulnerable to criticism. As Finnish composer Jean Sibelius said, "Pay no attention to what the critics say. A statue has never been erected in honor of a critic." Those who can't compete and succeed become critics.

LOVE THE GAME: COMPETE WITH PURPOSE AND PASSION

Whoever loves much, performs much and can accomplish much, and what is done in love is done well.

—VINCENT VAN GOGH

American soccer star Mia Hamm said, "Somewhere behind the athlete you've become and the hours of practice and the coaches who have pushed you is a little girl who fell in love with the game and never looked back. Play for her." Go back to your roots and your love of the game when you are experiencing a rough patch in your performance.

What is the point of playing sports, apart from earning a scholarship or salary, contributing to a cause, or getting fit? It's to have fun and to push yourself against competition. We all start out playing because we love the sport we are playing. When you are making a comeback, it's important to tap into this love and joy and to keep yourself motivated and engaged in the hard work that it will take to come back.

Enjoy the process and appreciate the moment. Before Derek Jeter played in his 14th and final All-Star Game, in 2014, the New York Yankees icon spoke briefly to the American League stars in the clubhouse before they took the field. This was Jeter's pregame speech.

It's an honor, it's a privilege to be here. To the guys and the younger guys who are getting the opportunity to come to their first, enjoy it. Because I can tell you first-hand that this is a fun experience. You should share it with your families, your friends—remember it. You don't know how many of these you're going to get an opportunity to play in. More importantly, remember every time you put your uniform on because, trust me, it goes quickly.

As Jeter said, understand that it's an honor and a privilege to play your sport. Take a moment to cherish the opportunity every time you put your uniform on. Be willing to roll up your sleeves and put in the hard work it will take to be the best you can be in whatever you do. Sharpen your sports skills to a razor's edge. Then put it all out on the field and leave it there. Lastly, remember that your big-picture goals will be reached by checking off acts of excellence on a daily basis.

The "fun" inherent in the word *play* is also a key. Pros *play* golf, *play* baseball, *play* basketball, *play* hockey, *play* volleyball, and *play* soccer. That's why we admire them; they *play* while others *work*. We don't say, "He works great at golf" or "She's a great worker in basketball." In actuality, the pros *work* really hard in practice, and this allows them to *play* their game at the highest levels.

Have as much fun as you possibly can while working *hard* and *smart* on your game in practice and spending time with your teammates and coaches. Think about positive practice or training sessions; don't goof off. Brazilian soccer legend Pelé said, "Success is not [an] accident. It is hard work, perseverance, learning, studying, sacrificing, and most of all, love of what you are doing or learning to do."

LEARN: EMBRACE A GROWTH MIND-SET

If I'm not doing it right, I want coach to tell me so I can fix it.

**—STEPHEN CURRY,
2015 NBA MOST VALUABLE PLAYER**

"Everyone is a genius. But if you judge a fish by its ability to climb a tree, it will live its whole life believing that it is stupid." Albert Einstein is credited with saying that. He's no fish. Everyone is intelligent—*in their own way*—and everyone can progress—*in their own way*—in all areas. All too often our education system seems to ask, "Are you intelligent?" It's something we ask ourselves as well, or maybe we go the other way and say someone else is dumb. But to be fair and to be wiser, shouldn't we ask, "How are you intelligent?" and "How can you improve?"

You have to discover your greatest, or champion, self. So explore your strengths, address your growth phases, and flourish *in your own way.* Enjoy the process of achieving your full potential in the sport(s) of your choosing. Remember this: Full involvement in what you deem most significant while achieving your personal best is your ultimate victory, even if you don't actually win the match, game, or trophy. In other words, you did your best and you still lost, but the takeaway is that you were beaten by a better opponent; you did not lose by beating yourself.

How do you approach sports, school, work, and all that you do? According to research by Carol Dweck, a professor of psychology at Stanford University, people face challenges with either a fixed mind-set or a growth mind-set. Someone with a fixed mind-set sees her abilities as they are, whereas a person with a growth mind-set views her abilities as changeable—for the better. Dweck contends that a growth mind-set is required to fulfill one's potential and maximize one's enjoyment of whatever one is doing.

People with a growth mind-set take ownership of the steps that bring success. They focus only on doing their best, whether on the field, in the classroom, or in the boardroom. Growth and development trump shortsighted win-loss records. Failure is just feedback, not something to be feared or fended off. People focused on growth regularly seek help to always keep learning and improving.

In contrast, a fixed mind-set is the proverbial dark cloud, shadowing all behaviors and limiting all achievements. People with a fixed mind-set are crushed by setbacks and struggles. They make excuses or play the blame game ("It's bad, but it's not my fault"). Mistakes are embarrassments instead of opportunities to learn. These players are fixed (stuck) instead of being fixers. Easy equals compromising, and it's easy to choose to avoid difficult or demanding situations.

How can we be champions if we don't take any chances? We have to embrace difficult and demanding situations and then learn equally from our successes and failures. Legendary UCLA basketball coach John Wooden said, "If you're not making mistakes, then you're not doing anything. I'm positive that a doer makes mistakes." Be a doer in all areas of your sport and your life by trying new things. Viewing safety as an overriding concern is for losers, not doers.

To move forward, recognize when you are succumbing to a fixed mind-set and switch gears to a growth mind-set. Ask yourself, which pattern am I in the following mind-set pairs?

FIXED MIND-SET 1: This new defensive scheme is too hard.

GROWTH MIND-SET 1: I will learn the new scheme by studying the playbook.

FIXED MIND-SET 2: I can't execute this skill.

GROWTH MIND-SET 2: I'm going to devote more practice time to honing this skill.

FIXED MIND-SET 3: I am so embarrassed by this mistake.

GROWTH MIND-SET 3: I will learn from this mistake.

FIXED MIND-SET 4: Coach is picking on me.

GROWTH MIND-SET 4: Coach is helping me become a better player.

FIXED MIND-SET 5: It's a loss.

GROWTH MIND-SET 5: It's a lesson.

FIXED MIND-SET 6: This setback is another stumbling block.

GROWTH MIND-SET 6: I will turn this setback into a stepping-stone.

FIXED MIND-SET 7: The other player (or team) is too good.

GROWTH MIND-SET 7: Playing against good players (or teams) is one of the best ways to improve my own performance.

FIXED MIND-SET 8: I'm jealous of my teammate for receiving all the accolades.

GROWTH MIND-SET 8: I'm proud of my teammate and even more inspired to elevate my own game.

FIXED MIND-SET 9: I should be able to make changes quickly.

GROWTH MIND-SET 9: It takes time and effort to build winning habits.

FIXED MIND-SET 10: If I have to work hard at my sport, I must not be very good.

GROWTH MIND-SET 10: If I work hard, I'll be a champion.

FIXED MIND-SET 11: He's tough and makes it look easy.

GROWTH MIND-SET 11: He worked hard; I'm going to work harder.

FIXED MIND-SET 12: Defeat is inevitable.

GROWTH MIND-SET 12: I can still make a play, win a point, sink a basket, or make a putt, in victory or in defeat.

During a journey, going off the map for a little while can be thought of as either leading to nowhere or leading to someplace new—someplace a little unexpected and maybe even more exciting. In the same way, a setback is like getting taken off your planned route. You can choose to reroute or assume you're never going to get to your destination. Embrace a growth mind-set and think of your comeback as a chance to reorient yourself and get back on course.

LABOR:
KEEP POUNDING THE ROCK

To give anything less than your best is to sacrifice the gift.
—STEVE PREFONTAINE, RUNNING LEGEND

Many athletes might see work as tedious, unproductive, and boring. In contrast, champions see work as a way to hone their techniques and move toward an ultimate goal and as a release from other daily pressures.

Many people mistakenly believe that successful people are just naturally superior to others. This is not true. In fact, people who master their work or sport are the hardest workers, in addition to being lifelong learners, as discussed in the previous section.

Gregg Popovich is the head coach of the NBA's San Antonio Spurs. "Pop" has been awarded three NBA Coach of the Year awards and has guided the Spurs to five NBA titles. He is a tough coach who earns the respect of his players, who gain internal fortitude by being a part of his hardworking system.

Like all champions, the Spurs have put in the requisite time and effort to achieve greatness. Pop uses the following quotation to motivate his players:

> When nothing seems to help, I go and look at a stonecutter hammering away at his rock perhaps a hundred times without as much as a crack showing in it. Yet at the hun-

dred and first blow it will split in two, and I know it was
not that blow that did it, but all that had gone before.

This encapsulation of Pop's blue-collar mind-set was written by
Jacob August Riis, a Danish-American journalist, photographer,
and social reformer. Sometimes pounding the rock requires grinding
through performance slumps and plateaus. Sometimes this involves
putting up with the boredom of repeating drills over and over.

The Italian Renaissance artist Michelangelo said, "If people
knew how hard I had to work to gain my mastery, it would not
seem so wonderful at all." Michael Jordan echoed Michelangelo,
saying, "Everybody has talent, but ability takes hard work." Former heavyweight boxing champion Larry Holmes understood this,
too, saying, "Hard work ain't easy, but it's fair." If you really want
to find out how great you can be in pursuit of your dreams, then
view the hard work as the first 100 blows on your rock.

What do coaches look for in prospective players? "I watch them
play and see who plays their butt off every possession," said Geno
Auriemma, the head coach of the University of Connecticut wom-
en's basketball team. He said this in 2015, on the eve of winning his
10th NCAA title with the Huskies. "They come down here, they get
a rebound, they outlet it, and they get a layup at the other end. They
run back, block a shot, and they just play like that the whole game."

Basketball superstar Diana Taurasi won three consecutive
NCAA titles with Coach Auriemma at UConn. She has also won
three Olympic gold medals with Team USA and three WNBA
championships with the Phoenix Mercury. What is her greatest
fear? "Knowing that the day has ended and I didn't work hard
enough," Taurasi said. "I want to know when my career is done
that I've put everything into it."

An uncompromising approach in training and continuous hustle in competition is vital to achieving sports-related goals. J. J. Watt is an NFL All-Pro defensive end for the Houston Texans. His willingness to embrace the extra effort required for excellence is one of the main reasons for his success. Here's what Watt says about working hard and representing yourself well: "I think no matter what job you do—I don't care what job it is—you want to outperform your contract. I feel like that's how everybody should attack their job, at least. You should want people to think you're underpaid because of how hard you work, because of how well you do your job, because of how you go about your business."

Take a moment for honest self-reflection. Are you outperforming your contract? Are you attacking your job on a daily basis? What about in your sport? Are you one of the hardest workers on your team? Put in 100 percent maximum effort toward your goals and bring a passion to the work. Be willing to put in the blue-collar labor rather than wishing you had more talent so that everything would come easily. It never will. The great ones make it look easy, but only after they put in the time and work.

LEARN OPTIMISM: BELIEVE IN YOUR COMEBACK STORY

Pessimism leads to weakness, optimism to power.

—WILLIAM JAMES, PSYCHOLOGIST

Optimism is a way of thinking about both triumphs and disasters. This psychological concept is belittled (by pessimists!) as being Pollyannaish or naïve. Others oversimplify optimism by comparing it to wearing rose-colored glasses, seeing the glass half full, or turning lemons into lemonade. However, the science of optimism shows that this concept is a part of healthy living and peak performance.

A review of the research literature reveals the numerous advantages gained by having a positive spin on life. Optimism is positively correlated with life satisfaction, happiness, and psychological and physical well-being. Optimists are less likely to develop cardiovascular disease, stroke, anxiety, and depression. Optimism also facilitates physical recovery among patients who have undergone surgery—something injured athletes should consider.

The positive psychology field has taught us about the benefits of optimism and happiness. One study correlated the life spans of Major League Baseball players with their smiles. In 2010, researchers Ernest Abel and Michael Kruger analyzed 230 baseball cards from 1952, a time when cards featured athletes looking straight at the camera. The results will make you want to smile.

- Players not smiling had an average life span of 72.9 years.

- Players partially smiling had an average life span of 75.0 years.

- Players with a full smile had an average life span of 79.9 years.

Players with a full smile lived an average of 7 years longer than their counterparts who did not smile. Moreover, several other studies looking at different populations also found that whether one smiles in photographs is correlated with happiness and longevity. These studies remind me of something Charlie Chaplin once said:

"I have many problems in my life. But my lips don't know that. They always smile." Chaplin lived to the ripe old age of 88.

How do you explain defeats, missteps, and setbacks to yourself? Martin Seligman, director of the Positive Psychology Center at the University of Pennsylvania and author of *Learned Optimism: How to Change Your Mind and Your Life*, describes how pessimists explain negative events to themselves as *personal*, *permanent*, and *pervasive*. Optimists are the opposite. They explain negative events to themselves as *situational*, *short-lived*, and *specific*. Here are some common sports examples:

PERSONAL VS. SITUATIONAL

PESSIMIST: "It is my fault we lost."

OPTIMIST: "They were tough opponents."

PESSIMIST: "I'm terrible."

OPTIMIST: "That was a challenging course."

PESSIMIST: "If something can go wrong for me this season, it will."

OPTIMIST: "I expect the best, and I'm prepared for everything."

PESSIMIST: "I always get stuck with a weak partner."

OPTIMIST: "I need to help my partner improve."

PERMANENT VS. SHORT-LIVED

PESSIMIST: "After how we played tonight, I bet we'll keep on losing."

OPTIMIST: "We had an off night, but we'll be ready to go next game."

PESSIMIST: "That team always beats us."

OPTIMIST: "We are learning what it will take to beat them."

PESSIMIST: "They always have bigger players on their team."

OPTIMIST: "We're going to make some adjustments to move the ball faster."

PESSIMIST: "We can never get our scoring going in the last quarter."

OPTIMIST: "We're going to bring in some fresh legs in the last quarter next game."

PERVASIVE VS. SPECIFIC

PESSIMIST: "I'm having problems with my hitting. I guess I'm in a funk. It will probably show up in my fielding also."

OPTIMIST: "I'm always only one at bat away from going on a hitting streak. Time now to play solid defense."

PESSIMIST: "I messed up that project at work today. Tonight's workout is just going to take it all out of me."

OPTIMIST: "I'll get that project straightened out, so let's put that in a box until tomorrow when I'm back at the office. In the meantime, my focus is on having a good workout."

PESSIMIST: "My teammate won't take the shot and it's messing up my timing."

OPTIMIST: "My teammate is off tonight, so I'll get a chance to take it to the basket more."

PESSIMIST: "There's no way I can find the time to do all of this. I'll get injured and there's no place to exercise. What's the point anyway?

OPTIMIST: "I'll make some slight adjustments in my schedule to get in some short workouts until I get stronger, then I'll work on some speed drills."

Does your self-talk explain negative events as personal, permanent, and pervasive? In my professional experience, many high achievers have an immediate, unrealistic, or negative evaluation of their performances. This often leads to or prolongs a slump. You will experience a letdown after a loss or other setback. Give it some time and then sweep those feelings aside and replace them with positive thoughts.

Remind yourself that the setback was an isolated event; it won't last long and it won't affect other parts of your life. Making excuses and failing to work hard should not be confused with optimism.

Putting a setback into context while continuing to train hard will help you bounce back, because you know you can do better in the future.

For example, imagine missing a personal-record lift during a training session. An optimist says, "Now I know what I have to do" (situational); "I just didn't have it today for this lift" (short-lived); and "The physical system is on for my next lift" (specific). In contrast, the pessimist says, "I'm not strong" (personal); "I'll never back squat 300 pounds" (permanent); and "I can never really excel at anything" (pervasive).

Flip the script after a positive performance to feel more optimistic. Say, "This is my real game" versus "I just got lucky"; "I did it now and I can do it again" versus "This probably won't last"; and "I'm going to bring this positive feeling into all that I do" versus "I'm only good at this one thing." Viewing victories this way will help you stay on a positive track because you know you made it happen.

A bit of pessimism (or realistically assessing the situation) can be valuable in certain situations. For example, if the consequences of being excessively optimistic are dangerous, such as ignoring a serious injury to continue playing, then err on the side of caution. Also, a bit of pessimism about your game can be helpful if your tendency is to become too reckless or uncontrolled in training or competition.

However, for long-term success and comeback journeys, optimism always trumps pessimism. What happens when you throw a brick at a window? The window breaks. What happens when you take a brick and add it to another? You build a house. Pessimists throw bricks at their dreams. Using bricks of hopefulness and confidence, optimists—champions—build their successful comeback.

LEAN ON YOUR MENTAL GAME: WIN THE GAME FROM WITHIN YOURSELF

In the sports arena I would say there is nothing like training and preparation. You have to train your mind as much as your body.

—VENUS WILLIAMS, SEVEN-TIME GRAND SLAM WINNER

Champions don't leave the mental game to chance or circumstance. As an athlete looking to improve your game—to play at your best more consistently, have more fun, and increase the chances of making successful comebacks—you will benefit from working on your mental game. To do so, practice these fun and effective mental training tricks.

• Develop clear and challenging big-picture goals.

• Maintain confident, upbeat body language to get the feeling of success in your body and mind.

• Visualize yourself making great plays and winning on the field, pitch, or court.

• Use positive, energetic language to motivate yourself into a winning mind-set.

• Breathe deeply, starting in your core.

Goal setting, body language, visualization, self-talk, and deep breathing are all part of getting where you want to be. Learn and master these beneficial skills for building confidence and gaining mental toughness. After they are ingrained, they become intuitive: What you do *now* lasts a *lifetime*.

Your mentality is the foundation of your game, and this strength is reflected in all aspects of your performance. You can fine-tune your game mentally and learn how to handle any kind of setback, such as a mental block, injury, or prolonged slump. Think of your mental game as something you can work on, just like your physical game. Growth in both areas will help you reach your greatest potential.

Improving your game is like stacking blocks. All of the following blocks are necessary for success:

MENTAL (e.g., confidence, concentration, toughness)

PHYSICAL (e.g., strength, stamina, speed)

TACTICAL (e.g., race strategy, game plan, course management)

TECHNICAL (e.g., skills, technique, mechanics)

Here's how it works: Pressure and stress get put on the stack of blocks during comeback attempts in big games or team tryouts, and if one block gets pushed out of the stack, then everything collapses. If the blocks stay strong and tightly bound together, then nothing can move or topple the stack!

Your stack of success will get stronger through intelligently applied hard work. Working on each block in practice will allow you to tower over challenges in competition. Every athlete can, and should, learn to win the game from within—that is, by thinking, feeling, and performing like a champion. The main difference between one's worst and one's best physical performance always hinges on one's mental performance. So start working on your mental game.

THE FINAL TAKEAWAY

Champions have a winning way of thinking about positive and negative events that helps them play to their full potential. View situations as challenges rather than as threats. Rely on supporters in addition to self-supporting. Maintain a growth mind-set in sports, work, and school. Focus on winning and learning rather than winning or losing. Refuse to be outworked or outhustled. See the positive instead of the negative side of things. All of these tactics will help you embrace, nurture, and fuel your comeback. Think of a full comeback and nothing less—bring out the best in yourself by learning from your setbacks and then looking ahead!

CHAPTER TWO

A CHAMPION CONTINUALLY COMES BACK

The real glory is being knocked to your knees and then coming back.
That's real glory. That's the essence of it.

—VINCE LOMBARDI

P icture a beautiful day in Tuscaloosa, Alabama, November 10, 2012: sunny skies and a warm 72°F perfect weather for college football. Top-ranked Alabama hosts 15th-ranked Texas A&M, with 101,821 fervent fans filling Bryant-Denny Stadium to the brim and a nation of football enthusiasts watching at home.

The Alabama Crimson Tide reigned as the defending national champions. They had accumulated a perfect 9–0 record so far, including impressive wins over No. 8 Michigan, No. 13 Mississippi State, and No. 5 LSU. But the underdog Texas A&M Aggies (7–2) had a plan, as they prepared to deploy a relatively unknown piece of their offensive arsenal: Johnny Football.

Redshirt freshman quarterback Johnny Manziel and the Aggies

exploded with a 20–0 first quarter, scoring on their first three drives. Alabama fought valiantly during the remainder of the game, but Texas A&M held on in the second half to secure the 29–24 upset win. This game launched Manziel into the national spotlight and propelled him on his path to winning the Heisman Trophy.

The defeat was devastating for Alabama. With a drop to No. 4 in the ranking this late in the season, the Crimson Tide's chance of making the national championship game seemed nonexistent. But Coach Nick Saban was undaunted: "The future and legacy of this team will be determined by what happens ahead of them, not what happens today or behind them."

Setbacks show a champion's true colors. Above all else, champions take pride in making comebacks; they relish the opportunity to come back stronger. They don't dwell on what they've lost. Rather, they learn from losses and focus on what they stand to gain, propelling themselves forward in a positive way.

Saban challenged the Crimson Tide to respond like champions, make the most of the remainder of the season, and accomplish everything that was in their power to accomplish. This required that they focus only on what they could do better and fully commit to doing better together as a team. Saban's challenge did not primarily concern outcomes. Instead, he challenged his team to focus on the process of becoming their absolute best.

Under Saban's commanding leadership, the Crimson Tide finished with energy and aggression, ending the season with a pair of 49–0 victories, over Western Carolina and Auburn. In the SEC Championship Game, they defeated the No. 3 Georgia Bulldogs 32–28, bouncing back from an 11-point third-quarter deficit.

This victory, combined with late-season losses by previously unbeaten Oregon and Kansas State, propelled Alabama to the 2013 BCS National Championship Game. The Crimson Tide rolled on to capture its 15th national championship by defeating No. 1 Notre Dame 42–14. Their glorious comeback to the top was complete.

Our legacy in sports and life will always be determined by how well we respond to defeat, downfall, and disappointment. When we get knocked down and get back up, we are truly champions—a lesson well proved by the 2013 BCS National Champions, the Alabama Crimson Tide.

SPORTS TERMINATORS

I'll be back.

—ARNOLD SCHWARZENEGGER AS THE TERMINATOR

In the first of a series of blockbuster movies, the Terminator, a cyborg assassin disguised as a human, is sent from the year 2029 back to 1984 on a deadly assignment. He is programmed to kill Sarah Connor. Sarah is a young woman whose actions, unbeknownst to her, play a key role in determining the future: She will give birth to the future leader of the rebellion against machines. Sarah's only protector is Kyle Reese, a human soldier also sent back from the war of 2029. The Terminator uses cyborg intelligence and machine capabilities to find Sarah. How can a simple waitress compete with this relentless cyborg?

In a now-famous scene, the Terminator attempts to con a desk sergeant into believing that he is a friend of Sarah's. The desk sergeant tells the Terminator to take a seat because Sarah is making a statement that could take a while. The Terminator examines the room and then says, "I'll be back."

The Terminator was released in 1984 to critical acclaim and commercial success. The movie starred Arnold Schwarzenegger as the Terminator, Linda Hamilton as Sarah Connor, and Michael Biehn as Kyle Reese. To date, five movies have been released in the series. The first sequel was *Terminator 2: Judgment Day* (1991), followed by *Terminator 3: Rise of the Machines* (2003), *Terminator Salvation* (2009), and *Terminator Genisys* (2015). The movies themselves keep coming back!

Champions are relentless competitors similar to Schwarzenegger's character in *The Terminator*. When he says "I'll be back," he means it! This persistence is one of the characteristics that makes the Terminator so terrifying: You can run, but you cannot hide. You think he's finished, but he keeps coming back time after time, never letting up or giving in. In sports, you want your opponents (or the situation) to believe you are a relentless Terminator. Kyle tells Sarah, "That Terminator is out there. . . . And it absolutely will not stop, ever. . . ." This persistence is one of the Terminator's characteristics that we, as humans, can emulate. We may not have cyborg intelligence and we may not have machine capabilities, but we *are* capable of persistence.

In your own game, don't stop until you've pursued (and hopefully achieved) your dreams and goals. This persistence—the ability to overcome adversity and come back even stronger, again and again—is what turns athletes into champions. Champions compete at their best when the opponent is hard-hitting or when the situation is demanding. So if you want to turn setbacks into comebacks, you should view tough opponents and demanding situations as challenges.

So are you ready to make a champion's comeback? Keep in mind it might be the hardest thing you've ever done. No one can make it easy for you. No one can provide you with a guarantee that you will make a successful comeback. You'll have to earn that honor by being as relentless as the Terminator as you pursue your goals with everything you've got.

Let's take a look at a few remarkable sports comebacks—athletes with their own Terminator-style stories. Find ways to relate each of these comeback stories to your own challenges. What lessons can you learn from these individuals? And remember, comebacks are not limited to sports; people come back in all areas of life. How do the following stories relate to your life, athletic and otherwise?

HOW THE OLDEST GUY OUTGUNNED THE YOUNG GUYS

The Americans? We're going to smash them. That's what we came here for.

—ALAIN BERNARD

On August 10, 2008, the Beijing National Aquatics Center—also known as the Water Cube—hosted the much anticipated men's 4 x 100-meter freestyle relay Olympic final. The French team of Amaury Leveaux, Fabien Gilot, Frederick Bousquet, and Alain Bernard were heavily favored. NBC announcers Dan Hicks and Rowdy Gaines told viewers that the Americans had virtually no chance against the French.

According to Gaines, "The French team, they are the favorites and they have been doing some talking. Alain Bernard, their world record holder in the 100 free, earlier told a newspaper, 'The Americans? We're going to smash them. That's what we came here for.' That article has been looked at by the Americans for extra inspiration. But it's going to take a lot, realistically, for the United States to out-touch France."

Michael Phelps, Garrett Weber-Gale, Cullen Jones, and Jason Lezak swam for the underdog Americans. In his third Olympics and already 32 years old, Lezak was the oldest male on the US swim team.

With Lezak going last for the Americans against Bernard, Gaines said to Hicks, "I just don't think they can do it. Jason Lezak has been there how many times in his career? Has he anchored this free relay?" Here's what Lezak later said about that race.

> Going into the race, we were the underdogs, and in the previous two Olympics we had been the favorite but come up a little bit short, so there was a lot of pressure going in there trying to get the US back on track for establishing our dominance in that race. It felt good being up against the French team that was talking some trash, too. The French team obviously had a lot of talent and they had four faster guys when you put their times down on paper. So we had to step up and swim fast.

The Americans started strong but fell behind the French in the third leg. Lezak then hit the water trailing Alain Bernard by half a second at the beginning of the anchor leg. I'll let Hicks and Gaines call the rest.

> The United States is trying to hang on to second; they should get the silver medal; Australia is in bronze territory

right now, but Lezak is closing a little bit on Bernard. Can the veteran chase him down and pull off a shocker here? Well, there's no doubt that he's tightening up! Bernard is losing some ground. Here comes Lezak! Unbelievable at the end! He's done it! The US has done it! He did it! A world record! Phelps's hopes are alive!

Riding a tidal wave of momentum, the 6'4" Lezak out-touched the 6'5" Bernard in a photo finish; only eight one-hundredths of a second separated the two teams. The US squad snatched the gold away from the French. Lezak had won the relay with the fastest 100 relay split ever (46.06 seconds). The American team catapulted past the world record by nearly 4 seconds, with a winning time of 3:08.24.

So how did Lezak do it? He later explained his thought process during his performance and how he avoided succumbing to negativity by using positive self-talk.

> When I pushed off the wall with 50 meters left . . . now the French guy's on my right-hand side, and I actually saw that he increased his lead on me and the thoughts going through my head at that point were, "Oh, no! No way am I going to catch this guy," as he's increased his lead and he's the world record holder.

But Lezak did not think negatively for long.

> I blocked those thoughts out and started talking over them with positive thoughts. As I kept doing that I felt really good, and I felt strong. I could see myself inching up on him, gaining a little space. By the time I got to about 50 meters left in that race, I felt this extra surge of

adrenaline that I've never felt before in a race. I always get that at the beginning of a relay and it wears off. Yet somehow, some way, this time I got that surge of adrenaline at the end of that race.

Sportsillustrated.com voted Jason's 4 x 100 freestyle relay anchor the most memorable single performance by an American at the 2008 Olympic Games. The race also won the ESPY Award for Best Moment. Lezak finished the 2008 Beijing Olympics with two gold medals and one bronze medal. In 2011, he competed in and lit the torch at the Maccabi Games in Israel. He then went on to win his eighth Olympic medal at the London Games in 2012.

COMEBACK LESSON: While the French team members were making brash statements to the media, Jason Lezak quietly focused on the challenge ahead of him. During the final leg of the race, he inevitably began to think negatively. But he refused to let these negative thoughts get between him and his remarkable comeback performance. He tried to ignore the negativity and turned up the volume on the positive thoughts that began to run through his mind. We can all learn to ignore automatic negative thoughts and replace them with positive thoughts. For Lezak, thinking positively had been a work in progress, and his efforts certainly paid off when gold was at stake.

As discussed in *The Champion's Mind*, negative thinking is like a Bad Wolf who is howling at us. All of us have an inner critic, our own Bad Wolf. During a comeback, we need to strive to keep our Good Wolf a winner by staying on a positive track when we hear the Bad Wolf creeping in, rather than tracking only the negative thoughts. The most important words you can ever say to yourself are *Stay Positive!*

With every thrilling victory comes a crushing defeat. The French then had to start their comeback. They didn't lose . . . they were beaten. The French 4 x 100 freestyle relay team made a remarkable comeback of their own in 2012 by winning the gold at the London Olympics.

EIGHT POINTS IN 8.9 SECONDS

I wanted to drive a stake through their heart.

—REGGIE MILLER

Reggie Miller played his entire 18-year NBA career with the Indiana Pacers. Miller was known for his deadly three-point shooting, especially in clutch moments. Many of his most memorable clutch shots came against the New York Knicks. At the end of his 18 years, he had made more three-point field goals than any other player in NBA history. A five-time All-Star selection, Miller led the league in free-throw percentage five times and won a gold medal at the 1996 Summer Olympics. On September 7, 2012, Miller was inducted into the Naismith Memorial Basketball Hall of Fame.

His most memorable comeback took place in Game 1 of the 1995 Eastern Conference semifinals against the New York Knicks at Madison Square Garden. The game appeared to be over, with just 18.7 seconds left and the Pacers trailing 105–99. These situations had become all too familiar for Miller, as the Knicks had eliminated the Pacers from the playoffs the previous two seasons.

But for Miller, the game was far from over. What happened in the next 8.9 seconds is now part of basketball lore.

The Pacers desperately needed someone to step to the fore-front. Miller obliged. He drained a three-pointer with 16.4 seconds left, immediately stole the errant inbound pass from the Knicks' Anthony Mason, sprinted beyond the three-point line, and then knocked down another shot to tie the score at 105 with just 13.3 seconds left in the game. Here is how NBC announcer Tom Hammond called the action.

> Miller for three, and he got it!
> Reggie Miller with a clutch trey, and it's 105–102.
> And a steal!
> Miller retreats to the three-point line and hits again!

On the next possession, the Knicks' John Starks was fouled by Sam Mitchell. Starks missed both free throws. The rebound of the second miss was grabbed by Knicks center Patrick Ewing, but he missed a 10-foot shot. Miller grabbed the rebound and was immediately fouled. He sank both free throws with 7.5 seconds left to play, giving Indiana the 107–105 lead. The Pacers would hold on to that lead and defeat the flustered Knicks.

"What shocked me was that Reggie had the presence of mind to not take a quick two-point shot and instead took one dribble and got back behind the three-point line to shoot a three," said Larry Brown, the Pacers coach, several years later. "That takes an amazing athlete to do that, a guy who literally has ice in his veins, a guy who loves the pressure and is willing to face the consequences if he doesn't make the shot." The Knicks had squandered their precious home court advantage and would eventually lose the series 4–3. The Pacers had been waiting, and they had now redeemed themselves.

COMEBACK LESSON: By making two spectacular three-pointers, getting fouled and fearlessly hitting two free throws (all net), as well as making a key steal and rebound, Miller displayed masterful performance and poise under fire to help his team grab a 1–0 series lead. As Coach Brown later mentioned, Miller was willing to face the consequences if he didn't make the shots. Miller later told the press, "If we lose, I'll take the blame. But I'll never feel defeated when I walk off the floor."

Play the same clutch way during your own comeback and don't get stressed out about the consequences of missing or messing up. *Just play to win.* Want the ball in your hands when it matters most. Like Miller, if you play to win, you can always cope with the consequences. Instead of feeling the pressure when things appeared hopeless, Miller turned up the pressure on his opponents, wanting to "drive the stake through their heart," and the Knicks crumbled. Always "be in it to win it" and keep putting the pressure on your opponent, regardless of what the scoreboard says.

"I SAW FIRSTHAND WHAT IT TOOK TO WIN"

I'm going to try and stay in the moment and be very patient.

—JORDAN SPIETH

Professional golfer Jordan Spieth, only 20 years old at the time, appeared to be in the driver's seat during the final round of the 2014 Masters Tournament. He held a two-shot lead over Bubba Watson but then sputtered on the eighth hole with a bogey as Bubba made a birdie. On the next hole, Bubba sped past him with another birdie and didn't look back on his way to winning his second green jacket, with a three-shot victory over Spieth and Jonas Blixt.

"I wasn't quite as patient today as I was the first three rounds and holding my emotions as well," Spieth said afterward. "I was very close. It was still the best I've ever done on a Sunday, and I know that it can only improve from there."

Even at such a young age, and only in his second full year on the PGA Tour, Spieth was clearly able to keep things in perspective. When asked how he felt, he responded, "So very excited, but at the same time [it's] a little bit bittersweet to come that close, and I truly believe that I will be back." Rather than obsessing over the negatives, he focused on the positives.

In true Terminator style, Spieth was indeed back in Augusta the following year, and in full force. He rented two homes during the 2015 Masters, one for socializing with family and friends and another just for sleep and rest. This is a good example of how he prepared and protected his mind and body.

Spieth shot a 64 on the first day to grab a three-shot lead. He increased his lead to five shots after 36 holes with a second-round 66. A third-round 70, which included a phenomenal performance on the 18th hole, gave him a lead of four shots over Justin Rose and five over Phil Mickelson.

On Sunday, Spieth played "Steady Eddy" golf by staying patient, positive, and process oriented rather than protecting the lead or pressing to force the result. He stayed within himself and shot a solid final-round 70 for a wire-to-wire win and his first major championship, tying Tiger Woods's 1997 performance for the lowest score in Masters history at 270 (–18).

Finishing second in 2014 helped Spieth stand taller in 2015. In fact, his most disappointing setback provided the opportunity for him to make his greatest comeback. Moreover, the worst "failure" of his burgeoning career had revealed to him that he could be a Masters champion. His loss the previous year taught him exactly what to expect and how to handle it better.

After Spieth's win, Tom Rinaldi of ESPN asked him how his experience the previous year had helped make 2015's result possible. His response: "I saw firsthand what it took to win. I saw what that meant after the tournament. I saw the legacy it left with Bubba, and I said that I want that. I said that's a desire of mine, that's a dream of mine from when I was really, really young. And it left a little chip on my shoulder. And when I got on the grounds this year, I just felt very, very comfortable from Monday on."

COMEBACK LESSON: Sometimes you have to suffer a devastating loss in a big event before you can win it. While undeniably gut-wrenching, the experience of finishing oh-so-close to a major victory can provide invaluable feedback not just about what you did technically or tactically that either worked or didn't but also about how you reacted mentally, emotionally, and physiologically in the live situation. You also get a firsthand look at what it took for your opponent to win it (i.e., to beat you).

Champions really do hate to get beaten, but they never fear it. Champions don't lose; instead, they force their opponents to excel and beat them. Being beaten by a superior performer is miles away from losing by beating yourself. If you're afraid of getting your heart broken, failing as you have in the past, looking bad in the eyes of others, or simply feeling uncomfortable in the spotlight, then you'll always beat yourself (or enable others to beat you) and never realize your dreams. So keep putting yourself in position to win and eventually you'll learn how to close out a game or tournament.

START WITH A DREAM
AND THEN OWN IT

*I've been dreaming about this moment since I was 12 years old.
It's a fairytale ending for me.*

—NICOLA ADAMS

A self-described tomboy growing up in England, Nicola Adams vividly remembers watching old footage of Muhammad Ali and Sugar Ray Leonard with her father when she was 12. Watching this made her want to win an Olympic gold medal one day, even though women's boxing was not included in the Olympics at the time. (Additionally, until 1996, women's boxing had been banned as a competitive sport for more than 100 years by the Amateur Boxing Association of England.)

Sadly, Adams's parents divorced, and her father and older half brother moved away. In the wake of the divorce, Nicola found solace in boxing. She explained, "I only went into a gym by accident. My mum couldn't get a babysitter and wanted to do aerobics, so she took me and Kurtis, my younger brother, down to the gym." There happened to be a youth boxing class that day, and Adams joined in. By the end of that first session, she was already eager to go back. "There weren't any other girls there, but I didn't mind," she said. "I loved it." The club gave her a sanctuary from the stress at home, helped her deal with the grief she experienced about her parents' divorce, and the people she met there became her second family.

"Even though women's boxing wasn't an Olympic sport then, I knew I would be an Olympic champion. Most people must've thought, 'It's never going to happen.' So I don't know why . . . it just felt like that was my path, and that one day I would achieve it.'"

In 2009, Nicola tripped and fell down the stairs at her home while rushing to get ready for a match. Despite this injury, she carried on and won her bout that day. Several days later, after enduring increasing pain, she learned she had broken a vertebra in her back. Nicola was bedridden for months and unable to train for a year. "I was worried I'd never walk again, let alone fight. That was scary," she remembered.

In 2011, Nicola won the silver medal at the World Championships, qualifying her to participate in the 2012 London Olympics, the very first to include women's boxing. The competitors fought in three weight classes: flyweight, lightweight, and middleweight. Standing 5'5" and weighing 125 pounds, Adams was in the flyweight division. She put her "home court advantage" to good use.

On August 8, Nicola faced Mary Kom of India in the semifinal match. Nicknamed "Magnificent Mary," Kom was a five-time amateur world champion and represented a significant test for Adams. In front of her home crowd, however, Adams had a spirited performance and won by a score of 11–6.

In the final, Adams faced Chinese boxing great Ren Cancan, then ranked No. 1 in the world. The southpaw Cancan had won three World Championships and had defeated Adams in the 2008 and 2010 World Championship finals. Cancan was considered the overwhelming favorite to win.

Adams started strong, and in the second round, she dropped Cancan with a powerful punch. Going into the third round with a big lead, Adams stayed aggressive and withstood a furious attack from Cancan to win 16–7. She accepted her gold medal as the home crowd roared with approval.

Adams's victory made her the first female boxer to win a gold medal at the Olympic Games. "It's like a dream come true for me," Adams said. "I've just wanted this all my life. To think I've finally done it with all this support. . . . I'd like to thank all the supporters here and support back home. I'm bringing that gold medal back to Leeds!"

COMEBACK LESSON: Adams's fairy-tale ending is still one for the ages. She overcame a serious back injury and two previous losses to her longtime rival to win a gold medal. Her comeback techniques included holding on to her Olympic dream in the face of doubters and surrounding herself with positive supporters. She didn't let all the naysaying about her personal goals or negativity about women's boxing faze her. "My family and friends are the only people I pay mind to," she said. "It's none of my business what anyone else thinks. I don't even know them, so why should I care?"

Like Adams, always continue to think big and never settle in your quest to be your best. When you suffer a setback, tap the power of your dreams and goals to help you make your comeback. Also, make sure to remember your role models, as Adams did with Muhammad Ali. Finally, surround yourself with positive supporters and disassociate yourself from negativity and naysayers.

Adams's fairy-tale story continued. In 2013, she was appointed a Member of the Order of the British Empire. She then added another chapter to her boxing legacy by defeating Michaela Walsh of Northern Ireland by split decision at the 2014 Commonwealth Games in Glasgow to earn the gold medal in the women's flyweight division.

SISU: FALL DOWN, GET UP

Get up, stand up, don't give up the fight.

—BOB MARLEY

The Finns have a proud distance-running tradition. For a small country, Finland has produced several superlative runners. In the 1910s and 1920s, Hannes Kolehmainen, Ville Ritola, and Paavo Nurmi were Olympic luminaries in mid- and long-distance events. Kolehmainen won four Olympic gold medals and one silver medal (1912 Stockholm, 1920 Antwerp), Ritola won five gold medals and three silver medals (1924 Paris, 1928 Amsterdam), and Nurmi grabbed nine gold medals and three silver medals (1920 Antwerp, 1924 Paris, 1928 Amsterdam).

Lean with a scruffy beard, Finnish middle-distance runner Lasse Viren made his Olympic debut at the 1972 Games in Munich, running both the 5,000-meter and 10,000-meter events. He was about to make Olympic history with one of the greatest sports comebacks of all time.

Racing at the fifth position, near the midpoint of the 10,000-meter event Viren inexplicably tripped, fell to the track, and landed hard on his back. "You really never are sure when it is happening, but your only thought is, 'Get up. Get up and race. Catch up to the leaders,'" Viren remembered. The whole thing happened so fast that Viren said later that he wasn't sure he started running in the right direction. Although his high-octane racing ability had been momentarily stuck in neutral, he got himself back in high gear and was determined to change the outcome of the race.

With an intensity that was equal parts desperation and inspiration, Viren made up the massive 20-meter deficit and grabbed the lead. The crowd was up and roaring as he zipped across the finish line 7 meters ahead of the silver medalist, Belgium's Emiel Puttemans. Viren set Olympic and world records with a time of 27:38.35.

Seven days later, Viren won the 5,000-meter event with a record-breaking time of 13:26.42. At the 1976 Olympics in Montreal, he achieved another Olympic double, conquering both the 10,000-meter and 5,000-meter events.

COMEBACK LESSON: Viren attributed his racing feats to a Finnish concept called *sisu,* a resilience and perseverance that can be expressed in the willingness to face and overcome incredible odds to reach one's goals. This "refuse to lose" attitude is the essential trait for all successful comeback performances in sports, as in other demanding endeavors.

As you think about these incredible feats, seize the opportunity to show your own sisu whenever you get knocked down, physically or mentally. Keep confidently moving forward no matter what happens or what's on the scoreboard. Viren's comeback is also a powerful metaphor for what you should do when life knocks you down. Remember this Japanese proverb: "Fall down seven times, stand up eight times."

THE MOTHER OF ALL COMEBACKS

I'm not really playing for the money. I just want to go out there and have fun. I really missed it so much last year.

—KIM CLIJSTERS

In 2005, after four Grand Slam finals losses, Kim Clijsters broke through to capture the 2005 US Open by defeating Mary Pierce in straight sets. In 2007, injuries forced the former world No. 1

tennis player with the powerful forehand to retire a month before her 24th birthday. Her retirement coincided with plans to start a family.

One year after the birth of her daughter, Jada, and 2 years after her retirement, Clijsters returned in 2009 for another round on the Women's Tennis Association (WTA) tour. She had missed the joy of the sport and the spirit of competition, and she appreciated tennis more than ever after taking the time to recover from her injuries.

In only her third tournament back, Clijsters played the 2009 US Open as an unseeded wild card. She went on a tear—winning big over Venus Williams, Li Na, and Serena Williams—to reach the finals against Caroline Wozniacki. Clijsters won in straight sets to complete her unlikely comeback and grab her second US Open title. Jada joined her on the court for the celebration.

Clijsters told reporters that she hadn't had any expectations about the outcome of the tournament upon entering, but the sports world was certainly surprised by Clijsters's title run in Flushing Meadows. Clijsters received the WTA Comeback Player of the Year and the Best Comeback Athlete ESPY Award. She continued to work hard on her game in 2010 and successfully defended her US Open title, beating Vera Zvonareva in straight sets. She was later named WTA Player of the Year and is the only person to win the Player of the Year Award the year after having been named Comeback Player of the Year.

Clijsters, however, still had one more Slam up her sleeve, winning the 2011 Australian Open title and her fourth Grand Slam overall by beating Li Na in three sets. She spent 20 weeks at the top of the WTA rankings in 2011. It was the fourth time Clijsters had been ranked world No. 1. However, Clijsters wasn't finished with the Australian Open or Li Na.

At the 2012 Australian Open, Clijsters cruised through the first three rounds before meeting up again with Li. In the first set, with the score 3–3, Clijsters sprained her left ankle. After a medical time-out, play continued with Clijsters hobbling. She lost the set 4–6. The second set came down to a tiebreaker. Clijsters was down four match points but won six consecutive points to take the second set tiebreaker 7–6. She held off Li with a decisive 6–4 third set to earn the match.

Despite her injury and falling behind to Li, Clijsters refused to submit. After the match, she shared the self-talk she used to will herself to her improbable victory. "I said in my mind, keep fighting. You never know what happens on the other side of the court." Clijsters would go on to defeat top-seeded Caroline Wozniacki before losing in the semifinals to eventual winner Victoria Azarenka.

COMEBACK LESSON: Like all champions, Clijsters got out of her own way during her comeback. Returning to competition after 2 years away from tennis, she didn't burden or limit herself with expectations. In the 2009 US Open, she had a "be prepared for anything" approach. She competed with an "everything to gain, nothing to lose" attitude because she was playing for her love of the game and love of competition. (This was her intrinsic motivation.) This helped her live in the moment and play her best.

Power your own mind and game with positive thoughts, and don't let others put a ceiling on your potential. Don't limit yourself with "realistic" expectations or place unnecessary pressures and demands on yourself and your performance. Rather than unraveling in the face of uncertainty, keep thinking, feeling, and acting like a champion. As Clijsters said, "You never know what happens on the other side of the court."

RELEASE YOUR MENTAL BRICK

You always recognize a great champion . . .
[by] how they come back from a loss.

—GEORGES ST-PIERRE

Georges St-Pierre, a Canadian-born, French-speaking fighter from Montreal, Quebec, worked his way to the summit of his sport from humble beginnings. He had a difficult childhood and was frequently bullied. Having played a variety of sports, he began training in kyokushin karate at the age of 7 to defend himself against bullies at school. The bullying soon stopped. Today, the Georges St-Pierre Foundation provides antibullying education and promotes physical activity in schools.

On April 7, 2007, the man known as GSP was on a fast track to becoming one of the greatest mixed martial artists of all time. In November 2006, he had claimed the welterweight title in dominant fashion by defeating Matt Hughes with a flurry of kicks and punches to the head resulting in a technical knockout. The victory also avenged the only defeat of his professional career to that time, a loss to Hughes 2 years earlier. GSP had rebounded after that first loss, reeling off six consecutive wins, downing his opponents with a well-rounded approach that incorporated freestyle wrestling, Brazilian jujitsu, boxing, and muay Thai. This superstar seemed unstoppable. Then St-Pierre lost the welterweight title in one of the biggest upsets in Ultimate Fighting Championship (UFC) history. Underdog Matt Serra pulled off the unthinkable, a technical knockout at 3:25 of the first round.

After losing the championship belt, GSP returned to training with a singular purpose: Avenge the loss. However, his obsession with payback against Serra was premature. He would need to fight a few other opponents before he would get another chance at the title. Since no win is guaranteed, it was important that he not become distracted by the ghost of Serra. GSP made good use of a popular sports psychology intervention. His mental coach advised him to "release his brick." GSP was weighing himself down with the psychological burden of the loss and needed to free himself and focus on his next fight rather than on avenging his loss to Serra. To get rid of this mental weight, GSP wrote MATT SERRA on a brick and tossed it into a nearby river.

According to GSP, this symbolic act released "a lot of the negative energy" that he was holding on to and helped him move forward. In his next fight, he won a unanimous decision against Josh Koscheck. He then beat Matt Hughes again via a second-round armbar submission.

St-Pierre had earned his rematch against Serra and was champing at the bit to get his revenge. The fight took place in front of GSP's hometown fans in Montreal. From the start of the action it was clear that the first fight was a distant memory. As the bout wore on, Serra began to crumble beneath St-Pierre's onslaught. The fight ended in a second-round technical knockout.

GSP had won the undisputed UFC welterweight championship for the second time, but he didn't let up. In fact, he was more determined than ever to keep the belt around his waist. He went on to win his next nine fights, improving his career record to 25–2. Many analysts proclaimed him the best pound-for-pound mixed martial artist during his winning streak. St-Pierre retired from the UFC in 2014, but he continues to train in the sport that is his greatest passion.

COMEBACK LESSON: Following his gut-wrenching loss to Matt

Serra, St-Pierre was able to recover, reflect, and reignite to move forward. After a major disappointment, champions feel what they need to feel and talk about what they need to talk about with their support team. A grieving process is often necessary. It should not be rejected or rushed.

However, St-Pierre didn't endlessly dwell on the loss by playing the "What if?" game. When it was time, he took to heart the words of his mental coach and let the past go. He then retooled his game using his mind and set his sights on making his comeback. Defeats and disappointments are an integral part of sports and life, but it's how well you respond to them that can make you a true champion.

LIVE INTO YOUR VISION

We must embrace pain and burn it as fuel for our journey.
—KENJI MIYAZAWA, POET

You have probably never heard of Tanner Gers. He grew up near Tucson, Arizona. He was a typical all-American kid who excelled in school and sports. He volunteered in the summer for Easter Seals and other organizations that served individuals with disabilities. A young entrepreneur, he worked in partnership with his brother washing cars, collecting aluminum cans, selling lemonade, and mowing lawns.

In 2003, personal stress and financial difficulties hit Tanner hard. Within 6 months, he lost his job, broke up with his live-in girlfriend, and had his car stolen. He had trouble paying his rent. Tanner slipped into a deep depression and self-medicated with alcohol. He was on a dark road and driving in the wrong direction.

After floundering for several months, Tanner decided that he had to turn his life around. He enlisted in the military. He found a temporary job. The police located and returned his car. He moved back in with his parents prior to being shipped off to boot camp. Life was once again moving in the right direction.

On the last Sunday of March 2004, he was driving back to his parents' home, located at the end of a dirt road, 45 minutes outside of Tucson. Tanner was coming around a corner when his car veered onto the dirt shoulder and flipped. The accident took Tanner's vision. It almost took his life. He was only 21 years old.

Two weeks later, Tanner was still unresponsive in the hospital. Among the long list of serious complications, he had developed a life-threatening infection in his brain. As the nurses prepared him for brain surgery, he gave a thumbs-up to his family. It was his first sign of responsiveness since the accident.

Tanner survived the surgery and made progress in the following weeks, but there were still many tough battles to be fought and many tough decisions to make. He lost one eye in the crash and was blind in the other. "If you are in the darkest room imaginable and then you close your eyes, that's how much vision I was left with," Tanner told me during an interview in the spring of 2015.

After spending several months in the hospital, Tanner returned to his parents' home to continue his recovery and rehabilitation. He was treated by a small army of medical specialists including his brain surgeon, a plastic surgeon, a neuro-ophthalmologist, an occupational therapist, and an infectious-disease specialist. He endured more surgeries and a battery of tests, including several MRIs and CT scans, over the next several months.

After Tanner was discharged from the hospital, his father found him hunched over at the table one day. "Head up!" he told his son. Tanner didn't respond. Sensing something was amiss, Tanner's father came over and sat down next to him. He asked what was wrong and if there was anything he could do for him.

"Nope, Dad, you can't do anything. I'm blind," Tanner replied.

"Tanner, I'm sorry, but that's not the attitude you need to have."

"Easy for you to say," Tanner thought.

His father continued, "Let me tell you something, Tanner. You should be blind and you should be in a wheelchair. In fact, you should be blind, in a wheelchair, and mentally disabled, Tanner. You should be a vegetable." He paused just long enough for his words to register and sink in and said softly yet sternly, "Tanner, you should be dead."

This proved to be the wake-up call Tanner needed. At that moment, he realized that everything he was going through could be far worse. "When you begin to understand that something that seems hard, difficult, or unfair is only a perception, then you can begin to realize something great. The greatness is that your entire experience begins and ends with a choice," Tanner told me.

He made the difficult decision to embrace his situation. "Sure, life's been more difficult without vision, but it's helped me become the man I am today. I don't know if I would be as good of a husband if that accident didn't happen. I probably wouldn't have developed into the leader I have become. I definitely wouldn't be the inspirational messenger or have the opportunity to make this type of impact if it were not for that single mistake."

In 2008, Tanner started playing blind baseball, otherwise known as "beepball." Tanner played well, and he enjoyed the competition, the teamwork, and the opportunity to play against evenly matched opponents. He enjoyed knowing that when he played, his disability didn't put him at any disadvantage. "That's when I really started working towards becoming the best athlete I could become in my life as a blind man," he said.

Tanner didn't just want to be an excellent athlete. Sports gave him a new purpose and sense of identity as a blind person after his tragic accident. Seeking new athletic challenges, Tanner decided to move on to track and field. In 2011, he joined a program called Arizona Disabled Sports with the goal of representing the United States at the Paralympics. Every weekend at 4:15 a.m., he boarded a Greyhound bus to make the 2-hour trip to train.

In 2011, he earned a spot on the US national track team. Tanner was also nominated to represent Team USA at the 2011 Parapan American Games in Guadalajara, Mexico. He won gold in the long jump and stood proudly on top of the podium with the US national anthem playing. Tanner's victory in Guadalajara qualified him to be on the Paralympic team. The 2012 London Paralympics featured 4,200 athletes from 160 countries who competed in 20 sports. Tanner Gers was among them.

COMEBACK LESSON: Following a near-fatal car accident and lengthy rehabilitation, Tanner returned to his love of sports and competition. He excelled in beepball and made a successful transition into track and field. His diligence and dedication paid off with a gold medal at the Parapan American Games and a trip to the London Paralympics. He is the founder and host of the Athlete Summit, a company devoted to helping others achieve greatness in sports and life.

By facing his comeback journey with the mind and heart of a champion, Tanner personifies the very best lessons that comeback stories have to teach us. He continued to seek out tough challenges, looked for opportunities to learn and grow, accepted help and support, put in the hard labor needed to realize his goals, and remained hopeful when the odds were stacked against him. It is easy to see that Tanner Gers is a champion.

THE FINAL TAKEAWAY

Every athlete presented in this chapter was criticized, doubted, and even given up on by others. Who expects a 32-year-old swimmer (Jason Lezak) to be the deciding factor in a young man's event like the Olympic swimming relays? Who believes in a young girl's (Nicola Adams) dreams to make the Olympics? Who thinks of a mom (Kim Clijsters) as a Grand Slam tennis champion? There is despair everywhere, but there is a champion within you.

These examples give us a glimpse into situations we will all inevitably face: defeat, setback, injury, and loss. What these sports champions have shown us is that there is a path to come back. Will you, like Jason Lezak, maintain positive self-talk to overcome overwhelming odds? Are you going to emulate Nicola Adams by dreaming big and ignoring the naysayers? Do you have a clear vision for your life's purpose like Clijsters, St-Pierre, and Gers?

The performances of these amazing athletes are tales of effort, persistence, and success. Each found a way to release his or her emotional brick and put energy into finding new motivation and drive. Embrace, nurture, and fuel your own comeback. Every one of these athletes went through weeks, months, and even years on a comeback journey. The key to a comeback is in a future full of hard work. Bring these comeback concepts into the reality of your life. After all, it's your game and your choice to be a champion. Your best is yet to come!

CHAPTER THREE

TEAM
TERMINATORS

There is something very valuable you gain when you've been
through tough situations. It's almost a surrender to the team.
You know you can't do it alone as it's got to be a group effort.

**—RUDY TOMJANOVICH, COACH OF THE 1994 AND
1995 NBA CHAMPIONS HOUSTON ROCKETS**

The German men's national soccer team won its first World
Cup in 1954 by defeating heavily favored Hungary 3–2,
despite falling two goals behind just 8 minutes into the contest. Hungary was the reigning Olympic champion and had not
lost a match in 5 years (32 contests).

The 2004 Boston Red Sox won eight games in a row to overcome
a 3–0 series deficit to beat the New York Yankees in the American
League Championship Series and then sweep the Saint Louis Cardinals in the World Series to win their first title in 86 years.

In the 2014 Sochi Olympics women's ice hockey gold medal game,
Canada was two goals down to the United States with less than
4 minutes remaining. Then Brianne Jenner scored at the 3:26 mark
to pull Canada within one goal. Marie Philip-Poulin then scored the
game-tying goal with 54.6 seconds remaining in regulation to stun

Team USA. Philip-Poulin won the game with a goal in overtime to complete Canada's dramatic comeback.

These major comebacks took chemistry, which had been developed by going through adversity. As Doc Rivers, head coach of the NBA's Los Angeles Clippers once said, "I don't know how you can pass a chemistry test without going through some adversity." When adversity strikes, will your team pass the chemistry test?

In this chapter, we will examine some remarkable *team* comebacks from which you can take valuable lessons.

- You will learn how to be an impact player and thrive as a member of your team.

- You will learn how to be a player who passes the team chemistry test and not one who brings everyone down.

- You will learn positive aspects of relationships and how to see red flags.

THE GREATEST TITAN TURNAROUND

Adversity is the fertilizer of growth.

—KEN RAVIZZA

Midway through the 2004 college baseball season, Cal State Fullerton head coach George Horton was frustrated. His team, which started the year ranked No. 4 in the country, was now halfway through the season with a dismal 15–16 record and was out of the top 25.

At his wits' end, Horton contacted Ken Ravizza, a professor who taught sports psychology courses in the university's kinesiology department. Coach Horton could see that the challenge for his team wasn't physical—it was psychological. He wanted Ravizza to speak to his players.

When Ravizza initially met with the team, the players were dejected and hung their heads. Ravizza simply said, "I don't know why you are feeling so sorry for yourselves. You have the chance to make the biggest comeback in Cal State Fullerton history."

Not having played a conference game yet, the players realized that Ravizza was right. By treating the rest of their games as if they were part of a new season, the team could still accomplish their big-picture goals: A conference championship and even a national championship both remained possibilities.

Ravizza worked with everyone in the program, from coaches to players. He worked with them during practice to ready them for actual games. He taught them mental skills and strategies for how to think, feel, and, most important, act like champions. His interventions also included unique environmental prompts, such as placing signs in the dugout (TAKE A "CHECK-IN BREATH") and implementing strategies that simply "flushed away" mental mistakes in order to focus on each individual pitch and moment.

Here are the strategies the 2004 Titans used, organized according to the Champion's Comeback Code:

- **LET GO:** To release their mental bricks, the Titans installed a miniature plastic toilet in their dugout. Instead of hanging on to errors or poor at-bats, the players pressed the handle of the toilet to flush away the negative play and refocus on the next pitch. To move on from a loss, the players gathered in a circle, took off their uniforms, and put them in a pile on the ground. Their emphasis now turned to the next game, the next opportunity.

- **LOOK FOR SUPPORT:** Not too proud to get help outside the program, Coach Horton built a winning team by reaching out to Ken Ravizza for sports psychology support.

- **LOVE THE GAME:** The players tapped into their love of baseball and began enjoying themselves. Their enthusiasm for playing the game returned.

- **LEARN:** The players embraced a growth mind-set, as demonstrated by their willingness to try something different. They understood that their situation was a golden opportunity to make the necessary changes to play to their full potential.

- **LABOR:** The players rededicated themselves to keep pounding the rock on a daily basis by working hard and smart.

- **LEARN OPTIMISM:** All of the players and coaches bought into their comeback story: Their new mission was to complete the biggest turnaround in Cal State Fullerton history.

- **LEAN ON YOUR MENTAL GAME:** The Titans started winning the game from within. They visualized success, practiced deep breathing, and used performance routines. As a result, the players were more confident and composed on the field.

These adjustments turned the Titans' season around. With a brand-new attitude and approach, they hit their stride at exactly the right time and started playing like winners. They compiled a regular season record of 36–20 that year, including a dazzling 19–2 record in conference play.

The Titans were awarded a host regional site in the NCAA Division I tournament. They won their opening-round game against Minnesota, but then lost to Pepperdine. Now facing elimination, the Titans beat No. 1 seed Arizona State 5–0. Next, they dominated Pepperdine twice to advance to the super regional round of play.

Once again playing on their home field, the Titans defeated Tulane twice to advance to the College World Series. With wins over South Carolina (2–0) and Miami (6–3), they advanced to the winner's bracket. South Carolina had advanced through the loser's bracket, which meant they would need to beat Fullerton twice to make the championship round. South Carolina won the first game 5–3, but the Titans returned the next day to win the second game 4–0.

Cal State Fullerton was back in the championship round for the first time since winning the title in 1995. The underdog Titans won the College World Series at Rosenblatt Stadium in Omaha, Nebraska, defeating the Texas Longhorns 6–4 and 3–2 to take the best-of-three series. They finished the season 47–22 overall. After their 15–16 start, Fullerton achieved their goal, completing the greatest turnaround in Titans' history.

COMEBACK LESSON: You won't win the "outer" game unless you play and win the "inner" game. The inner game should be at the core of your approach, as excellence always starts inside and works outward from the head and heart. Make the mental game an integral part of your performance.

Coach Horton brought in Ken Ravizza to provide sports psychology when nothing else was working for his team. Don't wait until the situation is desperate before making mental improvements in your own game and life. Grind harder and smarter to make a mental comeback and you'll reach your full potential and attain comeback success.

THE KINGS OF COMEBACKS

We never thought we weren't going to do it.
—DREW DOUGHTY

The Los Angeles Kings finished the 2013–14 National Hockey League regular season in third place in the Pacific Division and had to face the favored San Jose Sharks to begin the playoffs. After trailing three games to none, they won four consecutive games and captured the series. Next up were the top-seeded Anaheim Ducks. The Kings went down three games to two but then won two in a row to earn a matchup with the Chicago Blackhawks in the Western Conference finals.

Both teams battled their way to winning three games. Game 7 would send one team to the Stanley Cup final and the other team home. The Blackhawks turned up their game a notch and seized a two-goal lead in the first 9 minutes of Game 7. But the Kings would not be so easily shaken. "Two of their goals were pretty lucky, one from behind the goalie and the chip shot or whatever that was," explained Kings defenseman Drew Doughty. "We weren't going to let those kinds of goals defeat us. We knew that we were going to get them back, get some dirty goals from crashing the net. That's basically how we won the game. We never gave up."

Despite falling behind three times during the game, the Kings played with poise and came back to tie it each time. Regulation ended with the score at 4–4. In the 6th minute of overtime, Kings defenseman Alec Martinez scored the winning goal against the Blackhawks, the team that had won the 2013 Stanley Cup.

Los Angeles became the first NHL team to win three Game 7s in the same playoffs. All three series comebacks came on the road.

The Stanley Cup final would be the dramatic finale in an already historic comeback story.

The Kings clinched the Stanley Cup, their second in 3 years, with a 3–2, double-overtime win in Game 5 to take the series from the New York Rangers four games to one. As they had done so often before, they came from behind in three games during the series, all at home, and all culminating in overtime wins. "We made it a little hard on ourselves, but all you have to do is win," said Kings center Jeff Carter. "It doesn't matter how you do it."

COMEBACK LESSON: Rather than falling apart as the pressure began to mount, the Los Angeles Kings never gave up on their road to the 2014 Stanley Cup, earning a reputation as an all-time great team that never quit. Each time they needed an answer, they found one, no matter how improbable.

The Kings attributed their resilience to optimism and a strong culture of unity and commitment. They were a team that believed in and cared about one another. When adversity strikes, teams often break down and become individuals. But the Kings demonstrated outstanding leadership and teamwork. "We push each other," said center Jarret Stoll. "It starts with our head coach [Darryl Sutter]. He pushes us, and then we have a great leadership group and we push everybody. It just works."

"Character and leadership in the locker room," Martinez concurred. "We've got an unbelievable group in the room. [General Manager] Dean [Lombardi] has always said that we've got to be able to play hockey well together, but we've also got to like each other. All the guys in that locker room, we love each other. It's an unbelievable group." In your own game and life, don't pull apart when your team gets down; pull together like Kings.

KEEP CHOPPING:
THE FOREST WILL FALL

I will persist until I succeed.

—OG MANDINO, AUTHOR

On September 3, 2005, the University of Illinois Fighting Illini beat the Rutgers University Scarlet Knights in their first football game of the season—33–30 in overtime. During the third quarter, the Scarlet Knights had pulled ahead by 20 points. The comeback was unexpected, since Illinois was not exactly a powerhouse, having finished their previous season with a 3–8 record.

After the defeat, Rutgers's head coach, Greg Schiano, told his team they had to "just keep chopping wood. Right now we're in a bad spot. We're in the middle of the forest; it's all dark, we can't see. [So get] an axe and just start chopping away."

Schiano later told the media that he first heard the "chopping wood" mantra from sports psychologist Kevin Elko. This phrase is a powerful metaphor for proactively dealing with adversity. Rather than split apart, the players grew together as a cohesive team. The phrase resonated with Rutgers's students and fans as well. Students brought KEEP CHOPPING signs to the games, and the team's stadium became known as the Chop Shop.

"If you live by that motto, it can apply to anything in your life," fullback Brian Leonard, a future NFL player, explained to the media. "You get fired from your job, you just stay focused, you keep chopping and you get a new job. If you mess up on a play, you stay focused, put it behind you and look to the future, don't look to the past. That's what we do as a team now."

This lumberjack motto helped the players stay on target no matter what adversity they faced. After losing to Illinois, Rutgers won its next three games and finished the 2005 season 7–5, good enough for third place in the Big East. The strong finish earned the team a trip to their first bowl game since 1978.

In 2006, Rutgers again used "keep chopping" as their motto. They rallied from a 25–7 deficit to beat third-ranked Louisville 28–25 to cap a 9–0 run to start the season. The Scarlet Knights would go on to finish the season with an 11–2 record, including a 37–10 victory over Kansas State in the Texas Bowl.

COMEBACK LESSON: Panic is not an option for a champion. If your season gets off on the wrong foot, just keep chopping. If you fall behind in a game, like what happened to Rutgers against favored Louisville in 2006, keep chopping. Stay positive and proactive and you'll write your own comeback story.

There will always be spectacular victories and painful losses. Either way, champions keep chopping. If things appear bleak during your comeback, don't lie down and give up. Good things can and do happen when you keep chopping. Eventually, the forest will thin out and you'll find yourself standing in daylight.

TEAM UP: HOW CAN I BECOME AN IMPACT PLAYER?

The most valuable player is the one who makes the most players valuable.

—PEYTON MANNING, FIVE-TIME NFL MVP

A champion always respects himself and his sport. He shows respect to his teammates, coaches, and officials. What does it mean to respect your sport? Always put your best attitude and effort into competition. Play by the rules—at all times. Look for ways to help your team. Be sure to thank your parents, friends, and fans for their help and support.

"Un pour tous, tous pour un": "One for all, all for one." The Three Musketeers had it right! All members of a team should vow to support one other, both as individuals and as a group.

Nick Saban has coached his way to five college football national championships—one with LSU and four with Alabama. He understands the importance of mutual respect in building a winning team. Coach Saban said, "The number one thing on any team that will keep your players from being selfish is respect for the other players. Having respect leads to trust, and from that they begin to believe in each other. That is the way it works and that is the way it has to be."

Respect leads to better teamwork. Compete hard against teammates in practice, helping each other improve, and fully support one another in competition. There is a difference between positive rivalry and adversarial conflict. Establish the former, not the latter, with your teammates. Root for your teammates, even if you're on the bench.

Everything you do must be for the benefit of the team. Former NBA coach Phil Jackson said, "Good teams become great ones when the members trust each other enough to surrender the me for the *we*." So perform together in the spirit of teamwork—play by play, game by game. Seven-time World Series champion Babe Ruth confirmed this, saying, "The way a team plays as a whole determines its success. You may have the greatest bunch of individual stars in the world, but if they don't play together, the club won't be worth a dime."

A champion is an impact player. Champions help create an atmosphere of excellence that brings out the best in themselves and in others. They communicate in ways that help everyone stay positive and focused. Champions are the players who add to team chemistry; they are not the ones who cause unpleasant chemical reactions.

Good leaders find the best in others and help bring it out to play. In the words of five-time NBA champion Kobe Bryant, "Leadership is a responsibility. There comes a point when one must make a decision. Are *you* willing to do what it takes to push the right buttons to elevate those around you?"

"I like the responsibility that comes with being captain," said Ivan Rakitić, an attacking midfielder for FC Barcelona and the Croatian national team. "When my teammates aren't pulling their weight I raise the intensity of their performance with encouragement, and when they're getting carried away I calm them down."

Manu Ginobili, a four-time NBA champion with the San Antonio Spurs, is a shining example of a player who puts the team before himself. His willingness to come off the bench rather than start makes the Spurs more versatile and gives their second unit much-needed punch. "We have one goal. We don't care about who plays more or who has better stats because it's only about winning." A champion focuses on his teammates and does what's best for the team. The following strategies can help you become a better team player.

Understand the importance of bringing high, positive energy while showing good sportsmanship. Former world No. 1 professional tennis player Jim Courier said, "Sportsmanship for me is when a guy walks off the court and you really can't tell whether he won or lost." "When the last point is done, we are humans," concurred another world No. 1, Novak Djokovic. "Give your opponent a hug and say, 'Great fight,' and that's all."

To facilitate this feeling, it is customary among National Hockey League players to form a line and shake hands at the end of a grueling playoff series. College basketball and rugby players do the same. So should your team.

Speak affirmatively among your own teammates and avoid complaints and gossip. Accept individual differences. Each player is unique and has different strengths and weaknesses. Resolve problems with a teammate by talking privately and directly to him before they grow into something bigger.

Notify your coach if you are struggling with anything personal. This is the only way your coach can provide the support you need. Focus all of your energy on doing your best and helping your teammates have a positive experience.

Even though teams are composed of individuals with different roles, try to think of your team as one cohesive unit. Imagine each pitch, for instance, as thrown by the entire team, not just by the pitcher. If you happen to be the pitcher, don't let yourself carry all the responsibility or blame.

Debbie Miller-Palmore, a former Olympic and All-American college basketball player, said, "Even when you've played the game of your life, it's the feeling of teamwork that you'll remember. You'll forget the plays, the shots, and the scores, but you'll never forget your teammates."

What do you want to be remembered for?

BE A TEAM PLAYER IN YOUR RELATIONSHIPS

Shared joy is a double joy; shared sorrow is half a sorrow.
—SWEDISH PROVERB

At the 1986 Masters Tournament, 46-year-old Jack Nicklaus won his record 18th and final major with an electrifying come-from-behind one-stroke victory. In 2015, the US Congress presented Nicklaus with the Congressional Gold Medal for his stellar golf career and significant contributions off the course.

Nicklaus used this opportunity to recognize his wife: "People have asked me to quantify Barbara's importance in my career. I'd have to say she's responsible for at least 15 major championships. I'll give myself credit for 3." Healthy relationships off the field are crucial to achieving success on the field.

Having a healthy relationship is crucial because our relationships have a major impact on the quality of our lives. Fritz Perls, a noted psychiatrist and the founder of Gestalt therapy, summed up his approach to relationships in the "Gestalt prayer."

> I do my thing and you do your thing.
> I am not in this world to live up to your expectations
> And you are not in this world to live up to mine,
> You are you and I am I,
> If by chance we find each other, it's beautiful. If not,
> it can't be helped.

Think of your partner as complementing, not completing, your life. Don't try to change or control your partner, but support and grow with him.

In a healthy relationship, you appreciate that you are simultaneously together and apart. Time spent together doesn't feel suffocating, while time spent apart doesn't amount to isolation. Neither partner inhabits the role of savior or victim. Equal partners have a balanced relationship.

The positive aspects of a healthy relationship include the following:

• Openness and honesty—no major secrets or living double lives

• Genuine love and affection—both partners fully support each other when needed and compassionately challenge each other as necessary

• Fairness and equality—a true relationship is always a democracy, not a dictatorship

• Quality time spent together coupled with individual interests and activities—plenty of laughter, play, and fun

The red flags that you are in an unhealthy relationship include the following:

• At least one partner seeking to control the other

• Verbal or physical abuse

• Addiction to alcohol, drugs, pornography, or gambling

• Unwillingness to seek help or compromise when in conflict

• Minimal emotional intimacy or physical closeness

Enter relationships with eyes wide open and be aware of these positive aspects and red flags. Trust your gut and make sure to listen to your friends and family if they have strong (positive or negative) feelings about your partner. Don't let them make decisions for you, but take their views into consideration.

If you engage in abusive or addictive behaviors or you have a pattern of dating others who do, make every effort to address and work through these issues with help from a counselor. You are worth the time and effort this will take.

PRACTICE LIKE A CHAMPION TODAY

The time when there is no one there to feel sorry for you or to cheer for you is when a player is made.

—TIM DUNCAN, FIVE-TIME NBA CHAMPION

PLAY LIKE A CHAMPION TODAY, reads a well-known sign that every Notre Dame football players touches as he charges the field. The sign was put in place in 1986 by then head coach Lou Holtz, who led Notre Dame to the 1988 national championship and a perfect 12–0 record.

If you want to play like a champion *tomorrow*, then you have to practice like a champion *today*. Are you practicing to practice or are you practicing to progress? Practice is where champions are forged. Prove yourself in practice and then express yourself in competition.

Practice like a champion today.

Be *on time* and *on mind* (i.e., focused) for all practices and training sessions. Be physically and mentally prepared to be your best as soon as it's time to work. Minimize distractions. Turn off your phone. Develop and stick to a prepractice routine. For example, listen to music that amps you up or perform deep breathing to remove all distractions from your mind. Review your goals for added motivation.

Train your body in practice so that you can trust yourself in competition. In training, build your strengths and identify and work on your weaknesses. Simulate the demands of competition in practice so that on game day you will be able to trust your instincts to lead the way to victory. Trust allows your body to do what it has been trained and coached to do. "Train the way you will fight" is a boxing adage that you should adopt.

Practice the game so when you get to the game, it's just like practice. Unless you regularly bring your A-game to practice, you will not consistently have your A-game in competition. In other words, think less about trying to psych yourself up for the big game and more about how you will prepare for today's practice.

Champions take pride in their approach to practice. Commit yourself to doing your best no matter the task. Focus on the moment to the exclusion of all else. Work on all areas of your game and not just the things that come naturally.

Be mindful of your technique. In the words of Michael Jordan, "You can practice shooting 8 hours a day, but if your technique is wrong, then all you become is very good at shooting the wrong way. Get the fundamentals down and the level of everything you do will rise."

Remember, you don't do something until you get it right, you do it until you can't get it wrong. *Build solid mental and muscle memory!* Don't just practice a move or technique and stop when you do it right once after several attempts. Instead, when you do something right, practice until you can do it right consistently. Continued practice will make proper technique and form feel like second nature. That should be your goal for each and every technique. Effort in becomes effortless out.

Put into play all of your mental skills and strategies—think, feel, and act like a champion. Remember that each practice is a great opportunity to learn and get better. Cristiano Ronaldo, the 2014 FIFA Ballon D'Or winner as world footballer of the year, put it best: "If you think you're already perfect, then you never will be." Your goal is to always try to improve at every practice session.

PLAY LIKE A CHAMPION TODAY

At the end of the day you've got to feel some way.
So why not feel unbeatable, why not feel untouchable?

—CONOR MCGREGOR, UFC CHAMPION

By game day, many players have bloated bubble heads from watching film, listening to coaches, family, friends, enemies, and media. The smart ones ignore these distractions and focus on how they got where they are. The hay is in the barn: You've put in the training and practice to be here now, so *be here now*.

Enjoy the competition on game day. This will help you play your best. Think about why you play your sport and what you love most about it. Appreciate what's going on in the moment, because you've worked so hard to be in that moment. Relish the process and the race as much as the results.

Argentine footballer Lionel Messi said, "I continue to play the same way as when I was a kid. I have more responsibilities now, but I try to enjoy it as much as then." Fun with a purpose is how you play like a champion. If it isn't fun, why do it?

On the day of a competition, follow a mental preperformance routine. For example, spend a few minutes visualizing your performance. How does it look, feel, and sound? Try to see the images as

vividly as possible. Enlarge the image, brighten the colors, amplify
the feeling, and turn up the volume.

Olympic gold medalist Alex Morgan is a forward for the United
States women's national soccer team and the Portland Thorns FC
of the National Women's Soccer League. What does she do before
every game? "I put my headphones on and get in the zone and do
some imagery," she said.

Believe you can do it. Don't worry about your opponents' abilities and how well they are playing. Focus on *your* strengths and
what *you* can do to play your best; that's really all you can do. There
is no need to suddenly try something extra or different than what
you've worked on in practice.

Have you ever noticed that some athletes wither under pressure
while others thrive? Kobe Bryant, for instance, always wants the
ball when it's crunch time. Embrace the pressure; both sports and
life are about shining moments.

Athletes can flounder or flourish under pressure for a variety of
reasons. Some athletes don't put their best effort forward because
they fear failure and the shame and guilt it can bring. Others hold
back because they fear success and the increased demands and
expectations it can bring. Many players are so eager to win that
they press the action rather than perform within themselves.

All of these responses produce excessive muscle tension and
increased distractibility, which bottle up an athlete's talent rather
than allow it to flow in a natural, unrestrained way. As tough as
this may seem, especially at critical junctures, you have to be able
to let it fly (i.e., have no hesitation).

In terms of game strategy, play with measured boldness, not
reckless abandon, especially if there is a safe path to victory. Think
about the skilled tennis player who just puts ball after ball over the

net and wins by playing their best game. Or consider the smart golfer who aims for the middle of the green rather than impulsively shooting for a sucker pin placement. Be consistent.

To become a clutch player, practice to the edge in training: Treat a point on the scoreboard in scrimmage the same as you would in a playoff game. When the real situation happens, you'll have been there and done that in practice. Prepare like everything is on the line, even if you are just taking batting practice or shaping shots on the driving range.

It may be easier to slack off during a practice session in team sports, especially if the ball is not in your hands at a particular time. It's in your own best interest, however, in whatever position you're playing, to stay engaged 100 percent during practice. As they say, the best offense is a good defense. Keep those feet moving!

Have you ever seen a video of Michael Jordan looking defeated or ready to give up in a game? No way. On the other hand, have you watched other players yelling at themselves or cursing other players, and then said to yourself, "What a loser"? Their behavior is a reflection of what is going on inside (negative self-talk). Always stay in a winning frame of mind, regardless of the score or situation. Act like a champion to play like a champion; always maintain positive facial expressions and body language. This will say to the opposition, "You can't beat me mentally no matter what happens on the field."

Remember this: Clutch players hate to lose, but they never fear it. They know they have everything to gain. So always be in it to win it, whether you are on the practice field or playing for the championship. Sure, you'll lose a few games, but you'll win many more because you'll never defeat yourself.

Play any game and accept the outcome knowing that if you did your best, then you can hold your head up high. If for some reason you didn't, then there's the rub. Resolve to play your best next time. Retool your game in practice and return to competition a better player and team.

THE FINAL TAKEWAY

During times of great difficulty, team terminators pull together rather than split apart. Are you going to emulate the Cal State Fullerton Titans by transforming a disappointing start to the season into an extraordinary comeback? Like the Los Angeles Kings, are you going to keep believing in your teammates, especially when down in a game or a series? Will you "keep chopping" to move through hard times like the Rutgers football team by staying positive and proactive?

As a champion, constantly bring your best attitude and effort to your team, family, and relationships. There is everything to gain and nothing to lose when you do your best.

CHAPTER FOUR

MENTAL GAME
BOUNCE BACKS

The mind is powerful, and you have more control [of it] than you think.
—SCOTT D. LEWIS, CLINICAL HYPNOTHERAPIST

Your state of mind can take you one of two ways—up or down. Without mastering your mind, you risk losing before you even start. Mental focus is especially important after you experience a setback and need to regroup and recover physically and psychologically, whether that setback came from a loss, injury, or illness. The right state of mind can transform a losing performance into a winning one; it can turn a talented athlete into one of the best to ever play, no matter the sport.

In this chapter, you will learn tools that can help you win from within. You will learn how to master new effective strategies to get you through challenging periods in practice and competition. To become a champion, you must learn how to continuously bounce back from the following common mental game challenges.

• Mental clutter

• Distractions

- Motivational lags
- Inner doubts
- Negative thinking
- Muscle tension
- Performance jitters
- Anger

MENTAL CLUTTER

There are no ordinary moments.

—DAN MILLMAN

The 2006 movie *Peaceful Warrior*, adapted from Dan Millman's semiautobiographical novel *Way of the Peaceful Warrior*, tells the tale of a UC Berkeley student-athlete and his quest for Olympic glory. Dan is a star gymnast who seems to have it all until his leg is shattered in a motorcycle accident. A mysterious gas station attendant named Socrates, played by Nick Nolte, becomes Dan's mentor and guides him along his comeback journey to achieving personal excellence and peak athletic performance.

Mindfulness is one of the foundational principles that Dan learns to apply to his life. Socrates instructs Dan to "take out the trash" (mental clutter) that keeps him from being fully present in the moment. In other words, Socrates instructs Dan to let go of thoughts about the past and future and all other extraneous thoughts, to *be here now*. Socrates tells Dan, "That's the first part of your training, learning to throw out everything you don't need in here [pointing to Dan's forehead] that's keeping you from this moment."

What does this have to do with competition and peak performance? Socrates helps Dan understand that one can either focus on the competitive process or the outcome of competition. His advice to Dan is to "make every move about the move. Not about the gold [medal]. Not about what your dad thinks about you. Not anything. But that one moment in time."

In competition, there are many elements that you can't control. Referees will make bad calls, a spectator might yell and distract you, or you could twist your ankle. The possibilities are endless, and that is one reason we love sports, competition, and all of the excitement they entail. The best way to achieve success in competition is to keep your focus squarely on the process of performing your absolute best *all the way through*.

What is mindfulness? Mindfulness is a mental state in which one's focus is on the relationship between oneself and one's activity. Mindfulness benefits us by not allowing us to slip into autopilot—going through the motions of a movement rather than being conscious of what one is doing and why one is doing it. Mindfulness is perhaps best practiced, at least at first, while performing activities that do not require much mental focus, activities such as eating, sitting, or walking. Practicing mindfulness in these situations can help develop your ability to be mindful in other, more demanding situations.

As Sharon Salzberg, a Buddhist meditation teacher said, "Mindfulness isn't difficult. We just need to remember to do it." Here are some important ways to practice mindfulness. Make a point of doing them every day.

• **BRUSH YOUR TEETH MINDFULLY:** Feel the toothbrush, hear the sounds of the brushing, taste the toothpaste, and do not rush through it. This sets a mindful tone for the day.

• **SHOWER MINDFULLY:** Feel the water against your skin, notice the temperature, smell the soap. This provides a fresh start to your day or a way to rinse away negative "mental residue."

• **EAT MEALS AND SNACKS MINDFULLY:** Turn off the TV and put down the smartphone. Notice the textures, smells, and flavors of the food. Eat slowly and be in the moment.

• **DRINK WATER MINDFULLY:** Enjoy the refreshing surge as you drink water or a sports drink, feel it cool your chest, exhale/inhale to replenish your air.

• **DRIVE MINDFULLY:** Drive mindfully to class, work, the gym, and so on. Turn off the radio, turn off your phone to prevent distracting alerts, and pay attention to the road. Breathe deeply. You will arrive at your destination more refreshed.

• **STRETCH MINDFULLY:** Be in the moment while you stretch before or after physical exertion. Feel your muscles lengthening. As you hold the stretch, breathe into any tightness and exhale as you release a little bit more.

• **SIT QUIETLY AND MINDFULLY:** In your downtime, practice mindful meditation for 10 to 15 minutes. Put a cushion down on the floor or sit in a chair. Pay attention to your five senses. Let thoughts come and then let them go without attachment.

• **WALK SLOWLY AND MINDFULLY:** On the way to class, work, practice, or a competition, be in the moment rather than worried about what will take place after your walk. Breathe deeply, feeling your feet on the ground, and notice the wind.

• **BE MINDFUL AT PRACTICE:** Be all in, be all here. Put your gear and uniform on slowly and mindfully. Listen to your coach, and don't daydream. Practice as if you were in a competition.

• **STAY IN THE MOMENT ON GAME DAY:** As you prepare for a competition, bring the environment around you into focus, but don't worry about the outcome of the event. Stay in the moment. Raise your energy level. Keep in mind the words of University of Alabama football coach Nick Saban: "Focus on doing your job at the highest level, every single play, and the wins will follow."

DISTRACTIONS

Concentrate on what will produce results rather than on the results, the process rather than the prize.

**—BILL WALSH, HEAD COACH OF THE
SAN FRANCISCO 49ERS;
THREE-TIME SUPER BOWL CHAMPION**

Your focus can be on the past (the last play), the present (this play), or the future (the next play and beyond). But which of these options will contribute to optimal performance? The answer is focusing on the present! When you focus on performing, you're totally in the present. During competition, quickly learn from and then forget mistakes (the past) and don't worry about outcomes (the future). Focus on the present and remain purposeful so that you can own the moment and maximize your game.

The world's best athletes strive to be mindful in each moment. The results and outcomes can wait; you must remain focused on playing each play to the best of your ability. Here's how tennis player Rafael Nadal expressed it: "You just try to play tough and focus point for point. Sounds so boring, but it's the right thing to do out there."

During a performance, it's not your mistakes that matter; it's how quickly you recover from those mistakes. Don't give up physically or check out mentally when you make a mistake, error, or blunder. Keep your head in the game in the present moment. Focus on making one good play and doing your part, moment by moment, until the competition ends.

The competition may or may not turn out as you hoped, but either way, you did your best. You can live with the outcome knowing you gave it your all.

Athletes face many potential distractions, both on and off the field. Always remember that a distraction is only a distraction if you allow it to affect you. Do not let your attention be diverted. Ignore all negative thoughts and tune out the crowd in your mind. Instead, lock in on the task at hand, maintain a consistent breathing pattern, stay in the moment, and disregard disruptions by just looking away from them.

The positive effects of being in the moment extend well beyond sports. Let's say, for example, that you're watching a comedy and the jokes are coming at you fast and furious. You are cracking up so much that your stomach hurts. Then all of a sudden, your friend starts to gossip—*blah, blah, blah*. Because of this interruption, you missed jokes and punch lines and you are no longer focused on the comedy. Your enjoyment is squashed.

If you want to fully enjoy yourself and your situation, forget about the distractions and what you missed and enjoy the rest of the movie. The same goes for sports. If you want to enjoy yourself and compete at your full potential, then stay focused. Don't let distractions creep in! And if they do, quickly leave them in the past.

Focus makes everything more enjoyable. Keying in on your performance and focusing on doing your best in each subsequent moment is extremely gratifying. For example, if an infielder has just committed an error and then starts glancing at the stands or muttering this or that excuse, then it is unlikely she will be prepared for the next pitch. Instead, she should take a breath, feel the bounce in her legs, and be ready for the next play.

Find a word or phrase that helps you (and your teammates) refocus. Use this word or phrase to redirect your focus to your performance if you discover that your mind has wandered back to the past or skipped into the future. Here are some phrases that may help you refocus.

- "Snap back."
- "Be all here."
- "One play at a time."
- "We'll take the next one."
- "Let's go."
- "We got this."
- "All the way."

Our minds naturally drift or zone out; we're only human. Mental training allows us to notice this before it's too late and provides us with the tools to bring our focus back to the task at hand. With enough training and discipline, you will develop the determination to focus on the moment's challenges. Keep to the 3 P's.

- Focus on the *present*—what is happening this play, this moment.

- Focus on the *positive*—what you are doing well, your strengths.

- Focus on the *process*—what you need to do in order to be successful.

MOTIVATIONAL LAGS

For me the most potent motivational fuel was not ambition, I think, but curiosity. I wanted to see how far I could go.

**—CHRIS HOY, TRACK CYCLIST;
SIX-TIME OLYMPIC GOLD MEDALIST**

Motivation requires both passion and a goal. Different athletes have different goals—perhaps winning at the local club, or maybe winning an Olympic medal. Different goals require different levels of time, change, and commitment. A comeback is just another goal.

Think through your motivation. Are the goals driving you to play sports *personal*? Are you *internally* motivated? Some people play because their parents or friends want them to play. If this is the case for you, challenge yourself to play for yourself. What really fires you up and gets your blood pumping?

Look for ways to stay motivated and inspired as you pursue your big-picture goals. Motivation is the fuel that drives everyone, not just athletes, to accomplish feats they never could have imagined. And motivation is critical for keeping yourself on track when you inevitably encounter bumps along the road. Motivation is what all athletes need to stay in the fast lane.

There are two types of motives for participating in any activity: internal motives and external motives. Internal motives include the sheer joy of playing and the drive to continually improve. External motives, on the other hand, are those that come when you participate in a sport because you seek attention, awards, or praise.

To increase the odds of achieving your goals and to maintain motivation for the long haul, play your sport for its own sake, not just for any extrinsic benefits it may bestow on you. Think of external rewards as an added bonus. Play your sport because of the joy it brings you. Remember, if you don't enjoy the journey, chances are you won't enjoy the destination. Another way to sustain motivation is to realize that a minor setback is an opportunity to make a major comeback. After a hard fall or a tough loss, keeping a champion's state of mind will help you bounce back higher. Be determined rather than discouraged. Keep pushing relentlessly and confidently toward your goals.

Rather than becoming disheartened after a poor performance, get inspired about your comeback. "I'm the type of person that [doesn't get] down when I have a bad swim. I just get more motivated. I'm quite resilient in that way," said Rebecca Adlington, a world and Olympic 800-meter freestyle swimming champion.

To avoid motivation lags or a decrease in motivation, build a personal team of excellence by surrounding yourself with positive people. Have training buddies who push you and keep you focused and motivated. Share your goals with teammates you know will support you. Training buddies can keep you positive and working hard from beginning to end. They can help push you to your limits, which is how you'll improve. They can also make training fun. And that is allowed, too!

No matter what our specific goals may be, we all want to improve, and such positive change comes from effort. In contrast, negative change doesn't require effort.

Along the way, compile a "greatest hits" list of things that get you pumped. Inspiration might come in the form of something as simple as a song, a movie, a quote, or an image of your favorite athlete. Collect those things that get your heart racing and come back to them when you train.

Challenge yourself each day to fall in love with your sport all over again. Be on the lookout for a way to see your sport with fresh eyes, like you did when you first started playing. Find new ways to push yourself and improve. Again, writing down a phrase or two may improve your focus and give you a little extra boost to help you follow through with your plan. Try posting inspirational sayings or quotes somewhere you will see them frequently. This can help you stay on a positive track. Here are some winning phrases (along with their acronyms) for your consideration.

HBDYWI—How Bad Do You Want It?

MIH—Make It Happen

FOCUS—Focus On Controllables Under Stress

PACE—Positive Attitude, Complete Effort

MEDC—Make Every Day Count

Champions aren't simply dreamers. Champions are practical. They give their all, but they also listen to their bodies. Listen to what your body needs in order to train efficiently, avoid injuries, and prevent burnout. Sports psychologist Cal Botterill emphasizes an essential principle for all serious athletes: "Work is commendable, but recovery is essential."

Do something that recharges you. Rest days, social activities, hobbies, deep relaxation, and good sleep are critical for maintaining motivation. Naps are both physiologically and psychologically beneficial. Get your energy tank filled up for tomorrow by going to sleep early tonight.

According to US men's soccer goalie Tim Howard, "Athletes do so much to take care of their bodies, yet sleep is the element most get wrong." Howard takes an hour-long nap after each practice, and if he can help it, he is in bed by 10:00 every night. Howard knows how to give his body the downtime it needs to remain in top form—that's one reason he's a standout in his sport.

The mental grind of training and competing is often just as taxing as the physical exercise, so make time for both physical and mental regeneration. "Don't leave your fight in the gym" is a boxing adage well worth remembering. It means that you shouldn't overtrain and then underrecover. To keep your body powerful and your motivation high, make sure to "rest after you test." This will allow your mind and body to reset for your next training session and ensure that you stay sharp during competition.

INNER DOUBTS

If there is doubt in your mind . . . how can your muscles know what they are expected to do?

—HARVEY PENICK, WORLD GOLF HALL OF FAMER

Professional golfer Jason Dufner suffered a heartbreaking defeat to Keegan Bradley in a playoff at the 2011 PGA Championship at the Atlanta Athletic Club in Johns Creek, Georgia. Two years later he had another opportunity to claim his first major championship. This time he prevailed, winning the 2013 PGA Championship at the Oak Hill Country Club in Rochester, New York. After hoisting the Wanamaker Trophy, he offered insight into the frame of mind that carried him to victory: "I just decided that I was going to be confident . . . and try to win this thing!"

You must be confident in yourself and in your athletic ability to perform at your best, whether trying out for a team, competing for a spot in a starting lineup, playing against a higher-ranked opponent, rebounding from a poor start or a tough loss, or transitioning to the next level of competition. Identify the challenge, prepare yourself to conquer it, and then approach it with confidence.

Confidence is simple if you believe in you.

Novak Djokovic gave himself a much-needed confidence boost en route to defeating Roger Federer for the 2014 Wimbledon title. After losing the fourth set of the match, Djokovic went to the restroom and had a chat with himself. "I was loud to myself, saying, 'Believe in yourself!'" remembered Djokovic. "You know, it's not a cliché, it really works, even when you don't feel it, to say at times some positive things to yourself—that's exactly when you should do it." It's okay if it feels like you are faking it, at first. Fake it until you make it.

If you are confident, you can be your best when it matters most. Here are eight strategies for boosting confidence. Try them and see what works for you.

1. Give yourself a mental high five after executing a play or performance as planned. Positive self-reinforcement is like making a deposit in your confidence account.

2. Reflect on your past successes and highlights. This will lead to better play in the future. Replay these magic moments in your mind and feel how good they felt at the time. Later, when you need an extra boost, it will be easier to draw on these feelings.

3. Remember a particular occasion when you triumphed over a difficult challenge, such as overcoming fear in the face of a tryout or bouncing back from an injury. Write down some of the keys that made this success possible.

4. Think about the compliments others have paid you and your abilities. Remember what teammates, friends, coaches, and family members have said about your athletic prowess. They are the ones that know you and what you are capable of.

5. Mirror and mimic what your role models did to become champions.

6. Stand in a confident posture—feet apart, chin up, chest out, with a broad smile.

7. Repeat this to yourself prior to a competition: "I've practiced and I trust my training and preparation."

8. During key moments of a performance, command yourself to "Believe in yourself!"

Surrounding yourself with others who focus solely on winning and less on learning and development can undermine your confidence. If you are in an environment in which the feedback is negative and the criticism is destructive, find a more welcoming and supportive environment. You are more likely to flourish there.

It's about you. It really is. Have the confidence and sense of self to make and learn from mistakes. After you make a mistake, encourage yourself instead of beating yourself up.

Competition provides a unique opportunity to have fun while learning. There will be ample time to make adjustments before the next competition.

NEGATIVE THINKING

Negative thinking is almost 100 percent effective.

—BOB ROTELLA, SPORTS PSYCHOLOGIST

Do you let your thoughts and feelings get the best of you during practice? Are you kicking at the ball in disgust, cursing about this or that, making excuses left and right, and looking like you want to quit? If so, you're giving in to negative tendencies in practice that will return in important competitions. Don't practice negativity— practice the way you want to play!

Take a moment now to review your behavior in recent practice sessions and competitions. Did you drop your head and drag your feet after making an errant pass or missing a shot? By doing so you gave your opponents a chance to say, "We've got him now. He's tanking."

How is this performance affecting you? You know how!

If you are feeling or behaving negatively, it's because you are thinking negatively. Your body listens to everything your mind says. Thoughts, feelings, and behaviors are interconnected. If you engage in what I call "stinking thinking" on the inside, then it will show up in your outer performance. Positive self-talk will enable you to stay in a winning frame of mind and play your best, regardless of the score or situation. Negative thinking never leads to positive performance.

Champions stay positive, especially under pressure. Roger Federer has won a record 17 Grand Slam tennis singles titles. He attributes this, at least in part, to positive thinking: "I'm a very positive thinker, and I think that is what helps me the most in difficult moments."

It is vital to develop positive and powerful cue words and phrases to pick up your mood and elevate your performance—in competition, in practice, and as you go through your day. Put these cue words and phrases into play as soon as you notice that you are feeling mad, sad, or scared. There will be ample time *after* the game or event to fully process your feelings and talk about them with others.

Self-talk can be in the first person ("I've got this!") or the second person ("You've got this!"). In fact, research shows that self-talk can be more effective when you refer to yourself in the second person. Try it out to determine which type of self-talk is the best fit for you in different situations.

Keep your self-talk *positive* (optimistic and upbeat), *plain* (simple and straightforward), and *performance oriented* (focused on what you need to do to be successful).

Follow the example of Russell Okung, a Pro Bowl offensive tackle for the NFL's Seattle Seahawks. "There are so many [negative thoughts] telling you that you can't do something, but you take those thoughts captive, take power over them, and change them," said Okung.

Maintain a champion's attitude in your own game by switching off negative self-talk and turning on positive self-talk.

NEGATIVE SELF-TALK 1: "Oh, $*#@! I really blew that play."

POSITIVE SELF-TALK 1: "Next play, best play. I've got this!"

NEGATIVE SELF-TALK 2: "We are getting crushed! This is embarrassing."

POSITIVE SELF-TALK 2: "Stay focused—there's still more game to be played!"

NEGATIVE SELF-TALK 3: "There's no way I can do this!"

POSITIVE SELF-TALK 3: "I absolutely can do this!"

NEGATIVE SELF-TALK 4: "He's a cheater! My serve was inbounds!"

POSITIVE SELF-TALK 4: "It's just one shot. I'll just keep blowing serves past him."

NEGATIVE SELF-TALK 5: "The wind is messing up my game."

POSITIVE SELF-TALK 5: "Lots of wind, I'm going to up the spin."

NEGATIVE SELF-TALK 6: "These practices are lame. What's the point?"

POSITIVE SELF-TALK 6: "I don't care how far I have to run, these hills are mine!"

NEGATIVE SELF-TALK 7: "I blew that easy layup. How embarrassing!"

POSITIVE SELF-TALK 7: "Take a breath. I'll make my next shot."

NEGATIVE SELF-TALK 8: "I am so tired. Do we really have to do this?"

POSITIVE SELF-TALK 8: "My legs are on fire, this burn is awesome!"

NEGATIVE SELF-TALK 9: "I wonder if Johnny is going to ever get this play right?"

POSITIVE SELF-TALK 9: "I have to open up the field more for Johnny to make it an easy pass."

NEGATIVE SELF-TALK 10: "I'm down too far to win."

POSITIVE SELF-TALK 10: "I can win this next point (or make this next shot)."

NEGATIVE SELF-TALK 11: "I hate watching game film."

POSITIVE SELF-TALK 11: "My goal is to learn as much as I can. A negative attitude won't make it any better or easier."

MUSCLE TENSION

The goal is effortless power, not a powerful effort.
—BOB TOSKI,
PGA GOLF PROFESSIONAL HALL OF FAMER

I have always been fascinated by the way great sprinters seem to run with a sort of effortless power. This ease of movement best shows up in the super-slow-motion replays that follow real-time broadcasts. At this slow speed, you can see their tension-free face and neck muscles. You can even see the relaxed, full breaths they take.

Tension is the kiss of death for any athletic performance.

Extraneous muscle tension slows you down, saps your energy, and disrupts your mechanics, whether on the track, in the pool, or on the golf course. As golf instructor David Leadbetter put it, "Tension at address [before the club is swung], especially in the arms and shoulders, can kill a golf swing before it gets going." Byron Nelson (known as Lord Byron)—who won 54 PGA Tour events, including five major championships—knew this and suggested a way to address it: "One way to break up any kind of tension is good deep breathing."

Breathing rhythmically throughout your day can relax your body and help maintain peak energy levels. Inhale and expand your lungs for a 5 count and then exhale and relax your lungs for another 5 seconds. Relax your shoulders and jaw as you exhale. This activates your core. For increased mindfulness, notice how air feels cool as you inhale through your nose and warm as you exhale through your mouth. Listen to your breathing as you inhale and exhale.

When we are tense, our breathing becomes shallow and we sometimes even hold our breath. We can counteract stress and release tension, thus staving off these results, by taking a deep, centering breath from our diaphragm. This breathing exercise can be broken down into three simple steps.

1. Breathe in through your nose while you count to 5.

2. Hold for 1 or 2 seconds.

3. Breathe out through your mouth while you count to 8 (or try counting backward from 8 while you exhale).

Notice the exhalation is longer in this breathing exercise to further promote the relaxation response.

Give it a try right now and repeat the whole process four times. Do this prior to practice or competition to create a clear state of mind and a sense of well-being. It can help to think of your lungs as balloons. What colors are your balloons? Take in a deep breath to fill your balloons and let it out slowly and completely to empty the balloons.

Change your day for the better with a few deep breaths. This reduces fatigue, increases energy, and manages stress. Put a deep-breathing reminder into your electronic calendar. Place sticky notes with "Breathe" written on them where you will see them—on your textbooks, on your computer screen, or in your locker at school.

There are several ways to remind yourself to breathe in clutch moments, when the pressure is high. You might write "Breathe" on your sports equipment or uniform, such as under the bill of your baseball or softball cap, as a prompt to check in with your breathing and ensure that you are breathing fully and deeply. Making deep breathing a habit in practice and games will make it more likely that you do it in clutch moments.

"The team that breathes the easiest wins," said former Major League Baseball catcher Tim McCarver. Take a good, deep breath in competition prior to any significant activity: an at-bat, a free throw, or a penalty shot, for instance.

PERFORMANCE JITTERS

If I'm nervous, it means I had to work hard to get there. . . .
So I try to stop and be proud of getting to live in that moment.

**—MARIA SHARAPOVA,
WINNER OF FIVE GRAND SLAM TENNIS EVENTS**

Preperformance anxiety is one of the most common concerns that bring athletes into my office. Symptoms of anxiety include worrisome thoughts (e.g., "What if I lose?"), a dry mouth, difficulty breathing, a racing pulse, and an upset stomach ("butterflies").

The number one coping mechanism is understanding that pre-performance anxiety is how your body readies itself to perform at its peak! Just knowing that helps normalize performance anxiety. There is no way that you can physically perform at your best level without a moderate amount of physical anxiety. So let's recognize symptoms of anxiety for what they are without shame. We are only human, and being human is an anxiety-inducing condition.

Even though your opponent may look calm, he is likely experiencing a similar level of apprehension. As National Hockey League star Sidney Crosby said, "I don't think you're human if you don't get nervous." Act like a champion by maintaining positive body language even if you are feeling anxious on the inside. As we've already discussed, your body language can affect your mood and your mind.

Feeling anxious is not a pleasant experience, so we often try to get rid of anxious feelings. If we can't send anxiety away, sometimes we try to run from it. Neither strategy works. They both lead to *being anxious about being anxious.* The cycle can continue without end, so don't let it start. Smile broadly and breathe deeply to help get your butterflies to fly in formation in the *right way, right away.*

Margaret Hoelzer is a two-time Olympic swimmer and former world record holder. She won three medals at the 2008 Beijing Olympics: bronze in the 100-meter backstroke, silver in the 200-meter backstroke, and silver in the 4 x 100-meter medley relay. How did Margaret manage her anxiety on race day? Here's what she shared with me in a 2013 interview.

The best advice I have [for] athletes when I give talks is to control the controllables. You are in control of some things and not in control of others. Control what you can and don't worry about the rest. Also remember that you know what you are doing. You have done the race a thousand times. Even if it's the first time you are doing it in a meet, you've done it in practice. Swimming is nice in that it has certain things that will always be a constant: You will always be in a 25-meter or 50-meter pool. The flags will always be in the same place, and there will always be a black line on the bottom of the pool. If you get nervous, focus on the familiar things around you, remember that this is something you know how to do, and just let your body do what it's been training to do.

"Control the controllables" by developing and sticking to a routine and game plan. Don't worry about anything other than what you can control. Remind yourself that today is no different from yesterday or the day before that. Focus on the familiar things around you. Then let your instincts and training do their thing.

Make sure to keep your self-talk positive ("I know I'm ready and I'm going to cherish the moment"). We tend to rush when we are anxious, so breathe *slowly* and *deeply* and walk at a steady pace. Make sure to drink enough water. Do it mindfully. (How does it taste? Is it warm or cold?) Take the opportunity during time-outs or other breaks to steady yourself, bring back your focus, and breathe!

The more you ally with anxiety, the better you can make use of it to perform at your best level. Anxiety comes with a welcome surge of adrenaline, various natural boosters, and energy. The key is learning how to channel all of this into a winning effort.

The San Francisco Giants defeated the Kansas City Royals 3–2 in Game 7 of the 2014 World Series, winning their third championship in 5 years. Madison Bumgarner was named the World Series MVP for his masterful performance. He understands the importance of shrinking the game down to size (similar to Hoelzer's advice about treating competition like any other day) to perform his best—regardless of the magnitude of the situation. "As boring as it sounds, you've got to treat it like any other game," said Bumgarner. "For me, it's fun and exciting to go out there and get amped up and pumped up for the game. But I think a lot of people, when you do that, you don't play as good . . . as you should. So it's important to . . . just play good, fundamentally sound baseball."

As tennis player Maria Sharapova explains in the quote that introduced this section, you've worked hard to be in this position, so be proud. Tell yourself that this competition is a golden opportunity to display your talents and show just how good you really are. Control the controllables and treat a high-pressure situation like any other game. Free up your talent and go for it.

ANGER

The ballplayer who loses his head, who can't keep his cool, is worse than no player at all.

—LOU GEHRIG, HALL OF FAMER AND SIX-TIME WORLD SERIES CHAMPION

There are three basic types of anger in sports: self-directed anger (after you miss a shot), teammate-directed anger (when you sense they aren't pulling their weight), and "the world is out to get me" anger (when you sense referees aren't making the right calls or your opponents are cheating).

French footballer Zinedine Zidane is one of the greatest players in the history of the game. The attacking midfielder was named FIFA World Player of the Year three times and won numerous other awards for his accomplishments. Zidane led the French national team to victory on their home soil in the final of the 1998 World Cup, scoring two goals in a 3–0 win over Brazil and helping France earn its first World Cup title.

France returned to the final in the 2006 World Cup, and at the championship match against Italy, Zidane received the Golden Ball award as the best player in the tournament. Zidane scored the first goal of the game when he converted on a penalty kick just 7 minutes into the contest. Italy tied the game in the 19th minute when Marco Materazzi scored on Andrea Pirlo's corner kick.

At the end of regulation, the score was still 1–1, and the pressure-packed match continued into extra time. Near the end of that time, Materazzi directed trash talk in Zidane's direction. In response, Zidane lost his cool and used his head to ram Materazzi in the chest. He was immediately issued a red card. Playing the rest of the game without their star player, France was able to hold on until the end of extra time, but they eventually lost in a penalty shootout.

Zidane's display wasn't the first time, and it won't be the last, that an angry outburst by a player hurt his team. But with the World Cup hanging in the balance, it was one of the biggest mental blunders in sports history. Zidane allowed himself to see red and received a red card in return.

"Always keep your composure. You can't score from the penalty box; and to win, you have to score," said NHL Hall of Famer Bobby Hull. So how can you deal with anger when it strikes? What techniques are there to get your mind back in the moment?

Keeping your composure is the first step. The second step is motivating your teammates.

"Keep a blue head," is one of the mantras adopted by New Zealand's All Blacks, the world's most successful rugby team, for getting centered and maintaining composure in competition. For them, red signifies anger and other states of mind that aren't conducive to winning. Blue signifies an optimal, cool state of mind. Players have developed their own personal blue head triggers: stomping on the field to get "grounded" or focusing their vision on a particular place in the stadium.

Here are some blue head techniques for you to try.

• Walk away. Let go of the frustration and then get right back on target. No matter what happens (and crazy stuff happens in all sports), if you know you're angry, frustrated, or confused, walk away.

• Tell yourself to "stay frosty" or "iced" to remain cool and composed.

• Breathe slowly and deeply and think "r-e-l-a-x" as you exhale.

• Be mindful of the moment by focusing on some tangible sensations, such as the bounce of the ball or the coolness of the breeze, as the mind can't do this and focus on negative and intrusive thoughts at the same time.

• Imagine being in your favorite place.

• Remind yourself that your opponent is no different than you are, and if it's his or her day, then it's not your day. Part as friends.

Anger is often caused by an affront to one's beliefs about fairness. Cheating is more likely to spark your anger than whether a call was actually right or wrong. In the midst of an emotional situation, we won't always respond in the same way. Sometimes we will yell at referees, and sometimes we won't.

It's not just a (perceived) bad call that determines how you feel; emotions are not so simple. Remember, however, you have a choice about how you eventually respond to perceived injustices in all situations. Most important, the choice you make can impact how you perform, so choose carefully. Is getting worked up over one call going to help or hurt your chances of winning the game? Stay game focused; drop everything else.

In preparation for the unexpected, develop your own personal "heat of the moment" toolbox and keep it nearby. When you need it, you *need* it. In all sports (and in all facets of life), self-control is crucial, whether you're coming from behind in a regular season game or playing for a championship. We often feel impatient and irritated in these situations. These feelings are the prelude to a loss of self-control.

Play with an edge, but keep a blue head!

COMMON CHALLENGES

Opportunities to find deeper powers within ourselves come when life seems most challenging.

—JOSEPH CAMPBELL, MYTHOLOGIST

Mental toughness is the ability to remain positive and proactive even in the most challenging of circumstances. In fact, mental toughness is the primary mental attribute that all athletes should have. Remember, the idea is to seek out challenges, to build mental and physical muscles, and to get "comfortable being uncomfortable." When dealing with these common challenges, maintain a tough-minded, championlike attitude.

CHALLENGING SITUATION 1: Demanding schedule (athletic, academic, work, etc.)

CHAMPION'S RESPONSE: Focus on one task at a time. Concentrate only on school while studying or in the classroom; similarly, focus only on sports while practicing or competing. Use your refocus words and phrases ("Be all here!") when distracted or discouraged.

CHALLENGING SITUATION 2: Dealing with a significant injury

CHAMPION'S RESPONSE: Use all of your mental skills and strategies (e.g., positive self-talk, deep breathing) while adhering to your rehabilitation. Your long-term health and happiness is paramount. Champions know how to build a recovery team of trainers, physicians, and family. Stay connected with your teammates and talk about your feelings rather than keep them bottled inside. Cheer on your teammates from the sidelines. Learn as much about your sport as you possibly can.

CHALLENGING SITUATION 3: Performance slump or plateau

CHAMPION'S RESPONSE: Realize that tough times can make you even tougher because adversity builds an inner resolve. Never give up on yourself—remain patient and persistent. Speak with your coach and make necessary adjustments. Keep practicing. Something good *will* happen. You are always only one performance away from being back at the top of your game.

CHALLENGING SITUATION 4: Pressure to narrow your focus to a single sport

CHAMPION'S RESPONSE: Play a variety of sports rather than specialize in a particular one before you are ready to make a choice. It will improve your overall athleticism. Student-athletes often play a different sport each season. The objective is to become a well-rounded athlete, reduce injuries and burnout, and achieve long-term athletic success. Tennis legends Roger Federer and Rafael Nadal both played other sports before committing to tennis. LeBron James was an all-state wide receiver in football. Basketball greats Michael Jordan and Steve Nash played baseball and soccer, respectively.

CHALLENGING SITUATION 5: A sibling outshining you in sports or school

CHAMPION'S RESPONSE: Remember this: That's *your* brother or sister! Be proud of your sibling and cheer him or her on while continuing to focus on reaching your own personal and performance goals. If you are the person outperforming others, do not feel guilty about receiving positive attention for your accomplishments. As long as you earned the accolades and are graceful about winning, there is nothing for you to be sorry about. If you can, try to lift up those around you and help them rise to your level.

CHALLENGING SITUATION 6: Peer pressure to engage in risky behaviors

CHAMPION'S RESPONSE: "I'll pass." Keep repeating this statement until the message is received. No excuses or explanations are necessary. This steadfastness comes internally from self-respect and will benefit your game and life in the long run.

CHALLENGING SITUATION 7: Inclement weather or poor field conditions

CHAMPION'S RESPONSE: Make adjustments as needed and view the situation as a test to stay positive and focused on the goal. A competitive advantage is available to those who handle adversity better than the opposition. Be safe and have fun.

CHALLENGING SITUATION 8: Negativity from others

CHAMPION'S RESPONSE: Ignore the "noise" (in one ear and out the other), deflect comments with humorous statements ("Nice try!"), or assertively tell others that you won't stand for the negativity.

CHALLENGING SITUATION 9: Physical discomfort experienced during tough training

CHAMPION'S RESPONSE: Remember that you're not alone! Real teammates stick together. Think of the workout as a group effort—the presence of your teammates provides added power to stay strong. Educate yourself so you know the difference between pain that leads to gain, and pain that is telling you to stop.

CHALLENGING SITUATION 10: Playing against a former team or teammates

CHAMPION'S RESPONSE: Don't play down! They deserve your best game, so make sure to give it to them. Show them why you were such a great teammate. Be courteous and friendly, even if they aren't. Have fun!

CHALLENGING SITUATION 11: Playing an opponent you think has your number

CHAMPION'S RESPONSE: Play to win! Today is a brand-new opportunity to show how good you can play. They've had their run, now start one of your own. You've got nothing to lose!

CHALLENGING SITUATION 12: Boredom in practice (I just want to play!)

CHAMPION'S RESPONSE: Create game day–like scenarios in practice. Maybe your coach would be willing to implement drills that mimic game situations. It couldn't hurt to ask. Otherwise, introduce your own goals that keep you focused and working, no matter what your coach decides. For example, try to make every layup or dribble with your off hand.

CHALLENGING SITUATION 13: Distracted or unmotivated teammates at practice

CHAMPION'S RESPONSE: Take the lead to make practice more engaging. Set up some mini-goals for yourself and your teammates. Tell them you're going to run right past them on the next play. Challenge them to catch you.

CHALLENGING SITUATION 14: Coach doesn't put you in on game day or underutilizes you.

CHAMPION'S RESPONSE: Set up some of your own goals that don't depend on just one game. Work toward meeting those goals and wait for game-day opportunities to come. Put your energy into encouraging your teammates. There's no need to bring yourself or your team down. You're more than just a player—you're a champion!

CHALLENGING SITUATION 15: You are expected to carry your team to victory.

CHAMPION'S RESPONSE: Help lift all the members of the team and show them that you value them as much as they value you. Encourage one another and build each other up. Be sure to practice your mental skills for stress relief (e.g., visualization, deep breathing).

CHALLENGING SITUATION 16: Mistakes, errors, and blunders

CHAMPION'S RESPONSE: Learn from mistakes in practice, but overlook them during competition. Pat Summitt, former head coach of the University of Tennessee women's basketball team and an eight-time national champion, said, "Admit to and make yourself accountable for mistakes. How can you improve if you're never wrong?"

CHALLENGING SITUATION 17: Playing with a big lead

CHAMPION'S RESPONSE: Focus on the task at hand as opposed to anticipating victory. Never let up. Stay hungry.

CHALLENGING SITUATION 18: Negative thoughts about losing or quitting

CHAMPION'S RESPONSE: Champions don't really lose—someone has to beat them. Champions don't quit, either. Be tenacious in competition and gracious when you're beaten and realize that now you see clearly what you have to do to come out on top next time. Take time to assess your motivation. Making an informed, reasonable decision to move on is not quitting.

CHALLENGING SITUATION 19: Being in a situation in which your comeback is improbable

CHAMPION'S RESPONSE: Never give up! During the 1999 British Open at Carnoustie, Scotland, golfer Paul Lawrie started the final round 10 shots back, played well (his best, which is all he could control), and ended up in a playoff after Jean van de Velde had a triple bogey on the final hole. This is a case of never giving up and accepting that in all sports the improbable is still probable, albeit with a lot of help from others. Given a chance, Lawrie seized the moment and won the four-hole playoff.

CHALLENGING SITUATION 20: Down to the last serve, last swing, last point

CHAMPION'S RESPONSE: Sports history is full of great ninth-inning, two-out, two-strike homers; aces to return to deuce and stay alive; "unmakeable" chips or putts sunk at a major; and three-pointers made from half-court. Even 1 second, or a fraction of a second, is a lot of time in sports. It gives you a chance. Take it.

THE FINAL TAKEAWAY

To excel, you must develop the strength of will and resilience needed to defeat anxiety, frustration, distraction, boredom, and discouragement. This character trait—and knowing how to focus it—is especially important when setbacks show up, when injuries limit you, and when recovery is slower than expected.

You must learn to see these and other mental challenges from a different perspective—as competitors to be crushed. While gold, silver, and bronze only go to the top three performers in a competition, you can make sure you've done your best and take home a personal gold medal. Conquer all mental and physical challenges to stand on top of your personal podium.

CHAPTER FIVE

FITNESS AND ENDURANCE COMEBACKS

The only easy day was yesterday.
—MOTTO OF THE US NAVY SEALS

Sports can be difficult and even unforgiving. How then can anyone overcome the sense of intimidation at the start of a new sports season or when learning a new sport, returning to action after taking time off, trying a new workout, or braving high-intensity workouts (CrossFit, Spartan Races, or military training like that demanded by the Navy SEALs)? What is the champion's way to approach fitness and endurance challenges?

Some people psych themselves out by comparing themselves unfavorably to others. This can lead to avoidance or overtraining, either doing nothing or too much, too fast, and too soon. This chapter will give you the practical skills and strategies to conquer the unique challenges that come with trying a new fitness or endurance activity—and how to keep going strong!

BE A GOAL-GETTER

What keeps me going is goals.
—MUHAMMAD ALI

Champions appreciate the importance of setting goals. Goals are vital for creating motivation and for making sure you're heading for your target. Specific goals provide all athletes with success-driven focus and determination, customized to their abilities and objectives. As New York Yankees great Yogi Berra said, "If you don't know where you are going, you'll end up someplace else."

However, many athletes (or potential athletes) just go with the flow. It is as if they are on autopilot, without any specific, positive, or achievable fitness goals. For example, a student may hope to get on the varsity team or play on a team with her friends. She may rely on external factors, like her coach, to set team-related goals and expectations for each season. Others depend on their parents', friends', and others' expectations or goals. However, your goals should come from you. You should set your own goals, not simply accept them from others. As Canadian World Cup alpine skier Erik Guay, the 2011 world downhill champion, said, "First and foremost you have to do it for yourself."

As I described in my book *The Champion's Mind: How Great Athletes Think, Train, and Thrive,* champions think gold and never settle for silver or bronze. They have their own internal motivation to be the best and understand that maximizing their own potential is their ultimate victory. They know that while external support is important, they must first set some of their own goals.

So how good do you want to be? How much effort are you willing to put in to bring out your personal best? How much do you want, and what will it take, to be an athlete who is never complacent and strives to become the absolute best he or she can possibly be?

Diane Grant, an award-winning playwright and screenwriter, said, "It's better to walk alone than with a crowd going in the wrong direction." Setting personal goals will help you move in the right direction—*in your direction*. So don't just go along with your peers to get along. Decide what matters most to you, and do it!

Ask yourself, "What are my big-picture goals—not just in sports and fitness, but in life?" Then establish some daily, seasonal, and career goals that are challenging and reachable. Don't just *say*, "I want to be Michael Jordan (or Steph Curry or Carli Lloyd or someone else)." Concentrate on specific *daily goals* for improving your performance that you can work on step by step, day by day. Align these short-term goals with long-term plans.

Having an overall plan will also help to focus your energy, effort, and enthusiasm into measurable, potent change. How can you develop such a plan? Identify your big-picture goals (qualifying for the Ironman World Championship in Hawaii or earning an athletic scholarship, for example) and then write them down and put them in a prominent place where you will look every day. Use a fitness application on your smartphone. Load your plan files to the Internet cloud for access from anywhere. Post your goals on your favorite social media site. Research shows that when we write our goals down and share them with a friend, we can significantly increase the probability of achieving the desired result compared with when we only think about our goals.

Be as specific as possible. Champions understand the importance of increments (i.e., making steady, stepwise progress). Incremental goals eventually lead to larger goals. It would be unrealistic to wake up one morning and think that you can run a marathon if you have never trained for it. The most practical approach is to set a future goal and work backward to the present to determine the necessary increments. To get to the point where you can run 5 miles, you could run a mile a day for a week, 2 miles a day the next week, and so on, until you get to your 5 miles. Then start working your way to 10 miles. In order to get stronger and go longer, build mileage gradually. Then test yourself against your goals and make adjustments as necessary so that there is gradual, consistent, and achievable progress.

Young athletes are often very good at dreaming big and seeing their whole future ahead of them, but they don't really know how to break things down into simple, manageable steps. Therefore, in addition to identifying your big-picture goals, writing them down, and displaying them in a visible place, write out and post your action steps/incremental goals as well. For example, "run 1 mile" → "run 5 miles" → "race a 5-K." In fact, the more specific you are, the more achievable each step becomes. This puts you on a path of constant success and accomplishment.

A Chinese proverb worth remembering reminds us that "the person who moves a mountain begins by carrying away small stones." Similarly, legendary UCLA basketball coach John Wooden advised, "When you improve a little each day, eventually big things occur. . . . Don't look for the big, quick improvement. Seek the small improvement one day at a time. That's the only way it happens—and when it happens, it lasts."

Pursuing daily goals, such as practicing shooting drills for 60 minutes to improve your accuracy or studying at the library for 90 minutes to improve your study habits, learning retention, and grades, is how you make continual progress and ingrain lasting mental and physical changes. Doing something once has little lasting effect, but repetition creates muscle memory and habits that stick.

After you have set your plan in motion, with both big-picture and incremental goals, be sure to review all the things that are going on in your life and reflect on how this reality affects your overall fitness goals. Are you investing your time properly? Challenge yourself each day by incrementally hunting down your big-picture goals. In the words of San Francisco 49ers head football coach Chip Kelly, "Everybody has the same amount of time during the day, and you can either spend your time or invest your time." Invest your time wisely and build for the future!

To achieve your big-picture goals, you must overcome many daily distractions and obstacles. If your daily goal is to practice a particular drill, then you cannot let video games or other time-wasters grab your attention. What you accomplish *today* is what shapes who you are *tomorrow*.

Look at the science behind this. Imagine your goal is to keep track of a random 26-letter string such as *ailerhndiitllwditntdrbsefe*. Can you do it? This would be very difficult. Better yet, can you fit your goal into an established pattern, give it some structure, some meaning? One approach would be to just do one letter per day— do *a* today and then a*i* tomorrow and so on. Or perhaps you could take two letters each day. The alphabet is 26 letters long, and we all learned it somehow. This 26-letter string is no different. If we tackle it incrementally, we can easily memorize it.

Break your big-picture goal into smaller chunks. To become a varsity basketball player, establish some meaningful metrics: "This year I will be able to run 5 miles, hit 85 percent of my free throws, and dribble with both hands." These metrics are all key skill sets necessary to excel in basketball. You are not just practicing running around back and forth. Your mind is a powerful tool, so let it work for you today!

The next step is to focus on your process goals. That is, how to achieve your big-picture goals. At the beginning of each day, ask yourself, "What action steps will I take today to help me reach my big-picture goals?" Remember, today is *the* opportunity to pursue your goals!

Monitor your progress and update your goals if necessary. That is, take note of how you are progressing (where you are in the small steps) and consider if the steps or overall goal should be tweaked.

Get your fitness expectations in line with reality. Recognize the value of dreaming/aspiring, but always temper it with reality. Build steadily from your baseline fitness level. If the increments between the dream and reality are too large or ambitious, then failure and frustration are assured. Slow and steady progress always gets us closer to a goal! Here are a few things you need to look out for.

We all compare ourselves to others. This leads to disappointment; there is *always* someone better. Instead of comparing yourself to others, compare yourself *now* to the person you want to be *later*. You are unique, and your metrics, plans, and joys should reflect your own efforts, dreams, and accomplishments.

Is part of your plan joining a gym? Fitness centers can provide many new tools (expensive equipment, a focused environment, and social interaction), but they can also be intimidating. Change always brings apprehension. And when change involves bench-pressing 145 pounds as someone puts up 345 right next to you, it can be even more intimidating. Techniques for overcoming this kind of "gymtimidation" include:

• Setting clear short- and long-term fitness goals in tandem with a professional fitness trainer

• Engaging in positive, energetic self-talk ("I'm feeling good!") to motivate yourself and maintain a winning frame of mind

• Maintaining consistent breathing during your workouts to reduce tension and discomfort

• Displaying confident and upbeat body language (e.g., smile broadly and stand tall)

Daily routines help build consistency, and most elite athletes have routines that support their training regimen, including going to bed and waking up at a set time, forgoing time-wasters (e.g., surfing the Internet), and planning and packing balanced snacks before leaving the house in the morning. In contrast, if you do not maintain a regimen, you will have less fight in you to make it to the gym the following day.

Routines will help you stay present, own the moment, and maximize your workout. Elite athletes are mindful of being in the moment while exercising. For example, they make sure to consciously breathe evenly and deeply and monitor their heart rate (heart-rate monitors are important). They focus as much on process (maintaining correct form) as they do on product (how much weight they are lifting). If you are reading a magazine or watching TV while exercising, turn up your intensity level. Focus on what you're doing! Train your brain.

Pacing is very important. Looking too far down the road can lead to procrastination and avoidance. It can also lead to burnout and injuries. *Pace, don't race!* Focus on making consistent progress in your fitness regimen. Being able to pace yourself is part of the self-awareness necessary for change. Think about self-care basics, such as meal plans, sleep schedule, and time management. Are you aware of and taking care of everything that will allow your body and mind to respond and grow? First, ask yourself, How am I hurting my own cause the most (bad habits)? Second, ask yourself, What needs am I neglecting by engaging in my bad habits? Replace bad habits with positive actions. If you are emotionally eating to cope with stress, then learn and practice positive-thinking and deep-relaxation techniques instead. Relegate those negative thoughts and bad habits to a neutral corner.

Champions compete against themselves. They focus on doing their job and are not distracted by their surroundings. Set your own standards. Nonathletes can psych themselves out in the gym by comparing themselves to others. Often, they end up avoiding the gym or hurting themselves by trying to lift more than they should.

Here are some key mental strategies and tactics to give a real boost to your exercise regimen.

ACT THE WAY YOU WANT TO FEEL. How would you act if you were more motivated? If you lack motivation, such as when experiencing pre-exercise dread, act as if you *are* motivated. Putting those behaviors into your body and mind, even if they're forced, will quickly make them feel real.

DEVELOP A PREWORKOUT ROUTINE. Champions are physically and mentally prepared to be their best whenever it's time to train. Similarly, set the stage for success (listen to music that amps you up or meditate to remove all distractions from your mind) to reach a peak state of mind.

BE CONFIDENT. Champions focus on themselves. Don't worry about others' conditioning or fitness levels. Think about your strengths and what you need to do to accomplish your goals. Recall occasions in the past when you conquered a difficult workout, and think about how you did so.

OWN THE MOMENT. Champions always strive to do their best in the present moment. Likewise, don't allow yourself to get stuck dwelling on the past (What happened earlier today?) or skipping into the future (What do I have to do later today?). If you find yourself getting distracted, a great mantra to say to yourself is "Be all in, be all here!"

GIVE YOUR BEST EFFORT. World-class athletes are incredibly efficient. In the same way, periodically check in with your body during your workout to ensure that you are maintaining proper form, keeping breathing consistent, and sticking to your target pace. This will help you avoid injuries and maximize progress.

EAT RIGHT. Eat for both pleasure and performance. Make a meal plan and stick to it. Make a decision to eat mindfully by giving what and how much you're eating your full attention. Have a water bottle on hand to stay hydrated. It wouldn't hurt to write your fitness goals on the water bottle!

COMEBACK LESSON: The science of excellence tells us that in order to survive, our minds must simplify and automate the way we interact with the world. Consider driving: If you consciously think about your speed, the brake pedal, and what's in the mirror—all at the same time—you might not let your driving skills do their thing. The mind naturally wants to automate things. But are we all Michael Schumacher (seven-time Formula 1 champion)? No. There needs to be purposeful practice to make gains and get things into the automatic zone.

Be present and purposeful to own the moment, maximize your workout, and train your mind and muscles to perform automatically. Be mindful in practice so that your skills can be exercised spontaneously in games.

Engage your mind by focusing on growth phases. Are you just running on a treadmill or are you making sure you're fully extending your heel? Where is the edge you want to get past? Are you lifting up your knees? Are you breathing through your mouth or nose? Focus on improving your form—pump your arms faster and lift those knees higher! This is key to maintaining good form and maximizing energy.

Elite athletes focus on improving themselves. Ask yourself, "Am I the spectator or the one working out?" Identify your workout goals, create your plan, mind the details, and move closer to the top of the mountain.

FITNESS MOTIVATION

Nothing great was ever achieved without enthusiasm.

—RALPH WALDO EMERSON

Kim Chronister is a health psychologist and wellness and relationship expert. She is the author of *FitMentality: The Ultimate Guide to Stop Binge Eating—Achieve the Mindset for the Fit Body You Want* and *The Psychology behind Fitness Motivation: A Revolutionary New Program to Lose Weight and Stay Fit for Life*. I asked Kim to share three key suggestions for mastering fitness motivation.

VISUALIZE. Become visually inspired by following fitness models and trainers on social media and posting photos of your ideal body in your home. On a daily basis, visualize attaining the energy, health, and body of your dreams.

FOCUS ON YOUR STRENGTHS. It is essential that you remain positive to maintain fitness motivation. Reframe all negative thoughts ("I don't have the time") into more positive thoughts ("I will make the time, because workouts make me more effective in life and give me the energy and body I desire"). Reframing is a technique used in therapy, and evidence shows that it is highly effective in helping people function better in all areas of life, including sticking to a fitness program.

UTILIZE POSITIVE REINFORCEMENT. Frequent rewards are a necessary component of fitness programs. Reward yourself often and make sure these rewards do not sabotage your results by reducing your motivation. Some examples of effective rewards are shopping for new clothes, going to a spa, getting a massage, or going to a concert. If you find your motivation beginning to falter, plan a celebration months in the future. This will motivate you to work now.

COMEBACK LESSON: Kim has a positive outlook on fitness motivation. She sees rewarding yourself as part of the fitness program. Take the time to get a massage or go to a concert. Learn to enjoy the training, which becomes the best reward. Reframe any negative thoughts that come in and instead visualize the target state: a new you that is healthy, looking good, and filled with energy!

ROOKIE FITNESS COMPETITIONS

The human body is an incredible machine, but most people only get out of that machine what their mind allows them to.

**—RICH FRONING JR.,
FOUR-TIME CROSSFIT GAMES CHAMPION**

How do athletes brave a new fitness challenge? Champions are willing to take risks and try new things in order to be successful. Intimidation is a common reaction to new challenges. When intimidation is accepted and coupled with positive energy, fear transforms into a powerful jumping-off platform. Be willing to try the new, and win at it!

James FitzGerald believes in fitness through assessment, testing, research, programming, and more. He is the founder of OPEX and the International Center for Fitness. His 20-plus years of experience and service as a strength coach/technician and with nutritional- and lifestyle-balancing techniques, and his experience training other coaches, has made OPEX a sought-after method of bringing fitness to a higher order. When not coaching, he's a full-time husband, father, and fitness athlete. In 2007, he was crowned "Fittest on Earth," as winner of the CrossFit Games.

James shared with me seven key suggestions for conquering rookie fitness competitions.

1. Have fun, look around, smile often.

2. Less thinking, more doing.

3. Do not hold back. Be vulnerable and allow some magic to happen.

4. No one cares how you do. Really! So why worry? Be nervous and excited, not nervous and worried.

5. Full effort is full victory.

6. Chase the best, forget the rest.

7. Take each event one by one. Be present and don't look back or ahead.

COMEBACK LESSON: Entering a fitness competition involves taking a risk. But what do you risk? Bruising your ego. We pretend that losing is the end of the world. It just doesn't work that way. If we go out there and compete to make something big happen, without fears or doubts, as if we relish the opportunity, we can leave our egos on the sidelines. You can always learn and improve from one competition to the next.

Let yourself revel in the whole experience more. Include some family and friends, and have fun watching the other competitors. Tell yourself, "I'm just here to do my best and cherish the challenge. I don't feel pressure—I deliver it." At the end of the day, for most of us sports are about staying healthy and enjoying what our bodies can do. When you are at peak performance, it feels wonderful. Take some moments to savor that.

TRAIN SMART

He who stops being better stops being good.
—OLIVER CROMWELL, MILITARY COMMANDER

Tim DiFrancesco cofounded TD Athletes Edge, a company that offers a systematic, results-driven approach to performance training and rehabilitation. In 2011, he was named the head strength and conditioning coach of the Los Angeles Lakers. Tim earned his doctorate of physical therapy at the University of Massachusetts Lowell, after earlier graduating from Endicott College in Beverly, Massachusetts, with a bachelor's degree in science and athletic training.

I asked Tim to share common training mistakes competitive athletes make and ways to avoid them. Here's his response.

THEY ASSUME THAT BECAUSE THEY MADE IT TO THE TOP WITHOUT TRAINING THAT THERE IS NO NEED TO START NOW. Some athletes can make it to the top primarily on raw athleticism, talent, and potential. In this case, it can be easy to think that there is no need to train regularly given that it wasn't part of the routine on the way to reaching the highest level. The best way to avoid falling into this trap is to refuse to be satisfied with simply making it. Making it to the highest level of a sport should be viewed as an opportunity to someday be considered the best of all time. Athletes who recognize this as the start of a journey versus the end tend to leave no stone unturned, including making strength and conditioning a priority.

THEY THINK THAT IF THEY TRAIN TOO HARD OR TOO MUCH THEY WILL GET TOO MUSCLE-BOUND AND IT WILL NEGATIVELY AFFECT SPORTS-SPECIFIC SKILLS. This is a particularly popular belief in the sport of basketball, primarily among skilled shooters. Many believe that lifting hard, heavy, or often will change their shooting technique and affect their accuracy. A quick look at a list of some of the better shooters of all time can help correct this mentality. Ray Allen, Derek Fisher, and Steve Nash come to mind as great shooters who were not afraid to get in the weight room and push some weight around! These three sharpshooters made the connection between strength training and career longevity and took it seriously at early points in their careers. Additionally, they recognized that in order to get open or create their shots, they needed great strength, power, agility, flexibility, and balance—all of which comes from taking strength and conditioning seriously.

THEY FAIL TO ASSOCIATE STRENGTH AND CONDITIONING WITH INJURY PREVENTION. When working with competitive athletes of a high skill level, the goal of training should typically shift slightly from performance enhancement to a corrective/protective focus. The more bulletproof they can be, the more opportunity they have to help the team with their skills. Appropriate strength and conditioning strategies have been proven to help decrease injury susceptibility. Athletes who can recognize that strength and conditioning are about more than just performance/athletic enhancement tend to get more out of their training and are doing more to help their team.

THEY TAKE THE "ALL OR NOTHING" APPROACH. Some athletes believe there is little value in workouts that are not extreme in intensity, duration, and volume. These athletes, however, struggle to be consistent with training because it seems like such an investment to execute long and heavy workouts; so they skip days. To be truly consistent with training, understand that something is better than nothing. This takes mental toughness, but it is absolutely necessary. Committing to a program is important, even if you start with just 5 minutes per day.

THEY FORGET THAT IT IS IMPORTANT TO BE AN EDUCATED PARTICIPANT. I often see athletes who show up in the weight room and do the work but are on autopilot. If you are blindly following a plan without wanting to understand the plan, this shows a lack of investment in your body. If you are blindly following a strength and conditioning professional who truly knows what they are doing, the autopilot approach will likely not have negative results. However, blindly following a strength and conditioning professional who is also asleep at the wheel can be very bad! Avoiding this is simple: Show interest in the "why" aspect of your training. This does not mean questioning your coach or doubting their motives, but it does mean actively participating in your training beyond just the physical aspect. Any good strength and conditioning coach should welcome a back-and-forth dialogue regarding your training.

THEY DO NOT TAKE ADVANTAGE OF RESOURCES. Athletes often overlook excellent resources around them. They don't do this on purpose but often simply lack the resourcefulness to take full advantage of what is at their disposal. Many strength and conditioning or sports medicine staffs are full of experts within the industry who have a lot to offer. Think of it as a secret menu that you have to ask for in order to get the best meal. Sometimes the best tools are right under your nose, but you forget to use them. Athletes should challenge themselves to determine if they have really tapped into all the resources available, and if not, put them to use!

THEY VALUE TRAINING BUT NOT RECOVERY. Some athletes think that if training is good, then more training must be better! I will admit that this approach is a good problem to have, but it can develop into an issue if not managed. Athletes need to understand that high-level performance hinges on a tricky balance of the right amounts of training and well-timed recovery.

Picture the body like a bucket of water and stones that is filled very close to capacity. Training and recovery are like adding or subtracting stones to adjust the water level. Too little training, too few stones, and the water will drop below the ideal line. Too much training, too many stones, and the bucket will overflow. When the bucket overflows, good luck getting that water back in. More stones are not always better, and recognizing when not to add stones, or when to take a few out, is crucial to optimal performance.

Along with your training, pay attention to your mood, how you feel, and how you sleep. Difficulty sleeping, extreme soreness lasting longer than normal, and foul moods can all be signs of overtraining.

THEY VIEW TRAINING AS A PUNISHMENT RATHER THAN AN OPPORTUNITY. This is a major mistake, and it takes a big toll on what you get out of strength and conditioning. Typically, athletes who have a "training is punishment" mind-set end up doing the bare minimum, if anything at all. The flip side of that, and the solution, is a positive mind-set in which the athlete recognizes each training session as an opportunity to get stronger, bigger, faster, more bulletproof, and generally better at their craft.

THEY CRAM FOR THE BIG EXAM. Rest and time away from training is important. Some athletes take this to an extreme and don't train at all during the off-season. These athletes often show up for training camp expecting to use it as a way to "cram for the big exam," or, in other words, to get ready for the season in a week. This can result in injury or poor performance, which often results in becoming well acquainted with the bench.

The key to avoiding this scenario is to look at the off-season as an extension of the season. Make it easy on yourself by breaking the off-season into three blocks. In the first block, commit to training a minimum of 2 days per week. In the second, train 3 days per week. In the third, train 4 days per week. This should be manageable and have you prepared for training camp.

THEY START HOT BUT FINISH COLD. Any player can come into training camp with tons of enthusiasm and do all of the right things in the weight room during the first few months of a season. Few players, however, can do all the right things all season. There comes a point in every season, in every sport, where it feels like nothing is going well and the season is just dragging on. Athletes must anticipate this and weather the storm by being consistent with training. Finish what you started. One key to this is to determine the pace that you can sustain for an entire season and stick to it. That is far better than starting off the season setting records in the weight room and then fizzling out down the stretch.

COMEBACK LESSON: The key to getting the most from this list is to take small bites. Attempting to address each item on this list all at once could be overwhelming. Pick one or two strategies and slowly work on improving in those areas. Big results can come from seemingly small things!

ANIMAL SPIRITS: THE INSTINCT THAT GUIDES US

Spirit first, technique second.

—GICHIN FUNAKOSHI,
FOUNDER OF SHOTOKAN KARATE-DO

Jake Mace began studying martial arts at the age of 8 in British Columbia, Canada, with kyokushin karate. Jake has performed tai chi, yi jin jing, and other styles of martial arts throughout China, the United States, and Inner Mongolia, and he teaches tai chi and kung fu full-time in Arizona. His passion and life's work is teaching the Asian arts of healing and self-defense along with the dynamic and colorful Chinese martial arts styles.

Jake's goal is to continue pursuing his love and passion for the Chinese martial arts while instilling these values, along with a high level of tai chi and kung fu skill. His background includes various forms of physical conditioning such as Yueh Fei's 18-posture qigong, iron hand, and five-animal training. Tai chi chuan, pa kua chang, qigong, along with training in traditional Chinese weapons, are part of his Shaolin experience. He specializes in qigong meditation.

I asked Jake to share his perspective on sports, training, and fitness. Here's what he had to say.

Sports, athletics, and competition are three of my favorite parts of life! They are connected. From competition, sports are born. Humans have been motivated, by the pursuit of victory, to make themselves into some of the most athletic specimens the world has ever known. I believe that we love to participate in competition as well as watch competition because sports, competition, and athletics have the ability to awaken something in us that sometimes can become lost in life's day-to-day grind! I call that something our "inner animal."

The inner animal is the part of us that is wild. I believe modern-day society has the tendency to bury our inner animal deep within our heart, and as we become more technologically savvy, civilized, predictable, and overworked, that inner animal gets buried deeper and deeper. It is during a hard workout, during a competition that we desperately want to win, while watching our favorite team teeter on the verge of victory, or while watching another human being achieve the impossible that our inner animal is awakened and gives us feelings, hormones, the sixth sense, chi, and spirit, which allow us to feel that ancient feeling that all living animals, including humans, love to feel—the feeling of survival!

In Mandarin Chinese there is a word, *shén* (神). Normally this word translates into English as "spirit." I believe this ancient philosophical Chinese word is another way of saying "inner animal." Do you still have the ability to feel the shén? It is your animalistic fight-or-flight response. Shén is the ability to put yourself into the "zone" at will in sports, business, family, relationships, health, and fitness, or when trying to reach any other goals. Shén is the feeling you get when you know you did well and a great victory in your life has been won, be it for a gold medal in front of a billion people or quietly on your own with no one around! Victories can happen on any stage, and I believe that the people who know how to recognize, listen to, and tap into shén are at a great advantage when it comes to winning at life!

So often, the best athletes and competitors in the world must sacrifice so many things in order to reach the pinnacle of their skill and competitiveness. This quite often leaves them completely out of balance and out of focus with the rest of their lives! This is not shén. I believe in living a life of balance and having the ability to look inward into your heart, mind, and body in order to truthfully see yourself without filters.

Filters can blind you as to what is important in life. I believe that the world's greatest competitors and athletes are those who have the ability to feel shén and use it to succeed in sports, family, business, fitness, and relation-ships. Life is about achieving balance while you're alive so that you may one day die in peace. For every hour you put in at the gym conditioning your muscles, put an equal hour into a meditation to condition your emotions. For every hour you pour your heart, soul, and work ethic into your business, put an equal hour toward pouring yourself into your family. You must use every moment of athletic greatness that inspires you and awakens your inner animal or shén. Close your eyes, listen to your shén, and allow your inner animal to run wild every single day!

COMEBACK LESSON: "Animal spirits" was a term used by John Maynard Keynes when discussing his theory on economics and human behavior. It was a term to describe how emotions, instinct, and our own humanity can drive behavior and society. Jake Mace taps into something similar by describing the shén that he has found through martial arts to bring balance into his training and life. In fact, in modern life we can all too easily get ourselves boxed into a rigid set of rules, autopilot habits, and constant negativity. It's easy to become dulled by a constant flood of media and stress. Although it is important to make solid rational decisions about your training, rehabilitation, and goals, it is also vital to remember that motivation, drive, and passion can come from a deeper part of our psyche—the animal spirit. Don't forget to tap into this.

GO THE GREATER DISTANCE

My legs can keep no pace with my desire.

—HERMIA IN WILLIAM SHAKESPEARE'S
A MIDSUMMER NIGHT'S DREAM

Road-racing cyclist Greg LeMond won the 1986 Tour de France. The next year, LeMond was severely injured in a hunting accident. He made a remarkable comeback to win the 1989 Tour de France, overcoming a 50-second disadvantage on the last-stage time trial to outdo Laurent Fignon by 8 seconds. LeMond won the Tour again in 1990 to become a three-time champion.

During Chrissie Wellington's first-ever Ironman triathlon in 2006, her wetsuit flooded in the open swim and she had to be rescued by a kayaker. Wellington turned pro in 2007, and the rookie shocked the triathlon world by winning her first Ironman World Championship title at Kailua-Kona, Hawaii. She would go on to win the event a total of four times and set multiple world records.

In 1978, distance swimmer Diana Nyad, at age 28, attempted to swim from Cuba to Florida. She was unsuccessful. Nyad made three more attempts from 2011 to 2012. She failed each time. On her fifth attempt, at age 64, Nyad completed the historic quest by arriving in Key West 53 hours after launching from Havana. She said, "It wasn't so much what I want to do, but who I want to be."

Many people turn to endurance sports as a personal test, sometimes after a significant personal loss or as a heroic challenge. When your body is telling you it can't go any farther, is there a certain kind of mental hurdle that you have to get past to keep going? Is it only a cliché that "pain is a state of mind"?

SWIM, BIKE, AND RUN THE TALK

Until you face your fears, you don't move to the other side, where you find the power.

—MARK ALLEN, SIX-TIME IRONMAN TRIATHLON WORLD CHAMPION

Gloria Petruzzelli is a clinical psychologist with a specialization in sports psychology. A multisport athlete, Gloria has been competing in triathlons for 10 years. She has completed a total of 12 half Iron-man (70.3 miles) distance races and finished 14th in her age group in her first full Ironman (140.6 miles) at the 2013 Memorial Her-mann Ironman in the Woodlands, Texas. I interviewed Gloria in 2014 about what psychological techniques she uses on race day. She explained:

> As a sport psychologist and Ironman triathlete, there are key skills and mental strategies that are necessary for success. I attribute my best race performances, as well as my triathlete clients' best race performances, to these five key preparations.
>
> **1. VISUALIZE AND REHEARSE MENTALLY.** It is key for me to expect the best of myself but to also be prepared for the worst on race day. Almost all triathletes know that things can and will go wrong on race day, but it's how you manage the unexpected that matters. I use visualization/mental rehearsal skills to run through how I want my ideal race performance to unfold but also to help me prepare for what could happen. For example, I visualize how I will handle losing my swim goggles during the 2.4-mile swim or how I will handle my bike getting a flat at mile 80 or, what most often happens, what to do if I'm unable to hold down foods or liquids during the marathon (when a body is most stressed during an Iron-man). Visualization and mental rehearsal help me to prepare and to expect the unexpected. I also go into a race feeling more confident that I have prepared for the "what-ifs," so I don't have to worry about them until they happen, if they happens.

2. BE ADAPTABLE—MENTALLY, EMOTIONALLY, AND BEHAVIORALLY. I aim to be as adaptable as possible, which goes along with point number 1. I always keep in mind the work of Charles Darwin, reminding myself that it is not strength nor intelligence that promotes survival, but adaptability. This embodies what the best triathletes do throughout a 140.6-mile race. In order to get through the day with the least amount of suffering and pain, I must be willing to adapt to changing weather conditions and to adjust my actions according to the water, my body, my emotions, my bike, my nutrition needs, other competitors, the time, the race course, et cetera.

3. BE NONJUDGMENTAL AND OBJECTIVE. It goes along with point number 2, but if I am caught up in an emotional state or judging my performance, there is no space to problem-solve, and I might miss an opportunity to adjust to a better state. The best quote that I keep in mind is from Sarah Piampiano, a professional triathlete: "I don't think anyone ever has the perfect race. Whoever can problem-solve the best is the one who's going to win." This quote reminds me to *mentally* refocus and control how I interpret my body and the race conditions at any given moment so that I can quickly assess, treat, and keep moving forward.

4. BE MINDFUL AND PRESENT IN THE MOMENT. Being mindful during a race helps me remember that all things are temporary. This perspective helps me cope and also brings me relief from distressing emotions, judgments, or sensations that I have during a race. I will intentionally say to myself, "This will pass. This is only temporary. Time will pass and in 5 hours, 2 hours, or even tomorrow I will be in another place or feel something very different. So be here now." Mindfulness also helps me see each moment as separate from the previous, which works to any Ironman triathlete's advantage. I tell myself, "Be here now." When I am swimming, I only think about swimming; when I am on the bike, I only focus on the bike; and, likewise, on the run, I only focus on the run. It does me no good to think about the 112-mile bike during the 2.4-mile swim. This will likely overwhelm me. Mindfulness allows me to be fully engaged in my moment and relieves me from distressing thoughts.

5. CONDUCT A NONJUDGMENTAL EVALUATION OF YOUR PERFORMANCE. When it's all said and done and announcer Mike Reilly says, "You are an Ironman!" it is so imperative that I have a balanced perspective on my race performance. It's very rare in triathlons that any athlete has a perfect day, but triathletes, myself included, are very hard on themselves. We have a difficult time giving ourselves credit for the aspects of our race we executed well. I try not to evaluate my performance until a few days after a race, when my body and emotions have stabilized and recovered from the 11-plus hours of racing. This will hopefully allow me to see my performance as feedback and home in on areas that I can improve upon. We triathletes are very competitive within ourselves. We thrive on breaking mental, emotional, and physical limitations, and *that* is definitely worth giving myself credit for.

COMEBACK LESSON: As we have seen from Gloria's words of wisdom for competing in a triathlon, it is important to mentally rehearse both optimal and adverse situations. The response to these situations is to be adaptable and nonjudgmental. The old saying still holds: "All things will pass." Stay focused on what needs to be done to finish a race. And when all is said and done, first give yourself time to decompress postrace before reviewing the performance. Take enjoyment from your accomplishments!

TO INFINITY AND BEYOND

Every single one of us possesses the strength to attempt something he isn't sure he can accomplish.

—SCOTT JUREK, ULTRAMARATHONER

Bryon Powell is an ultramarathoner, the author of *Relentless Forward Progress: A Guide to Running Ultramarathons*, and the publisher of the outstanding trail and ultrarunning Web site iRunFar.com. Ultramarathoners compete in distances of 31 miles, 50 miles, 62 miles, or even 100 miles. I interviewed Bryon in 2014 about how he moves through the wall of pain and discomfort to achieve the goals that rest on the other side. You don't have to be an ultramarathoner to benefit from his advice.

> **1. BREAK THE RACE INTO PIECES.** Egad, an ultramarathon is a long way! If you start thinking about the fact that you've got 30, 50, or 90 miles left, you'll be intimidated no matter how many ultramarathons you've run.

A good plan is to work from aid station to aid station. That's comprehensible. Late in the race, you might be focusing on getting to the next tree.

2. PLAY MNEMONIC GAMES TO HELP YOU REMEMBER YOUR NEEDS. Whether you're relying on a crew, drop bags, or simply the aid stations for supplies, use word games to remember your needs so you remember them when the long expanses of alone time abruptly and jarringly end at the frenetic flurry of an aid station. When a new need comes up on the trail, I pick one word to describe that need. I repeat this step for each of my subsequent needs, each time rearranging the words into a catchy phrase.

3. MAKE IT FUN . . . FOR EVERYONE. If you're running along with someone, start singing with them, to them, whatever. When you come to an aid station, crack a joke, get the crowd going, whatever. When those around you smile, you smile.

4. SMILE LIKE YOUR LIFE DEPENDS ON IT! Forget the studies. I know when I'm smiling, I stay in my happy place longer, and that means I run better for longer. Some of the most extraordinary ultrarunning performances I've seen this year were by runners consciously trying to smile, to enjoy themselves, to stay in a better mind-set.

5. WONDER . . . WHAT IF? Whether it's on a training run or in a race, I like to let my mind wander into what-if mode. Even with my all-to-often negative brain, the what-if thoughts buoy me. No matter how ridiculous or fantastic, they've never been a detriment.

COMEBACK LESSON: Bryon's advice as an accomplished ultra-marathoner can be summed up in one line: Smile like you mean it! Smiling helps you keep your mind focused on a positive mindset. Fun is contagious and gaining positive energy from others is important in a battle against ultralong distances. Use mnemonics to remember what you need, and break up the long distance into manageable segments. Do all this and you'll be smiling at the finish.

HIKE THE TALK

Hike Your Own Hike (HYOH).

—OFTEN-QUOTED APPALACHIAN TRAIL PHRASE

Zach Davis is the author of *Appalachian Trials: A Psychological and Emotional Guide to Successfully Thru-Hiking the Appalachian Trail.* Approximately 70 percent of the 2,000 people who attempt to thru-hike the Appalachian Trail each year fail to reach their goal. How was Zach able to overcome the mental and physical obstacles to go the distance and accomplish his mission? Here's what he shared with me.

1. MAKE YOUR GOALS PUBLIC. Making my goals public was the most important part of the goal-setting process. Positively stating my goal (I am going to thru-hike all 2,180 miles of the Appalachian Trail) to every single person who would listen to me was a huge factor in my finishing the trail. On the days where my feet were covered in blisters, when I was getting caught in vicious thunderstorms, when my knees were sore and my head aching (I contracted West Nile virus approximately 1,000 miles into the trail), never once did I consider throwing in the towel. Knowing there were hundreds of people who would have thought less of me, the embarrassment of doing so would be far more painful than anything the trail could've thrown my way.

2. ENDURE MENTALLY AND EMOTIONALLY. It was important for me to not only set a goal but to specify definite reasons for why I needed to achieve it and what I would think of myself if I didn't follow through. In *Appalachian Trials*, I encourage readers to make three lists: 1) why they're thru-hiking, 2) what they expect to get out of the experience, and 3) what will happen if they quit on themselves. It's a bit more elaborate than the previous sentence indicates, but in a nutshell, I encourage (*read:* threaten) aspiring hikers to really dig deep and uncover compelling emotions to convince their future selves that they absolutely can't quit. It can be an uncomfortable process, but it pays huge dividends.

3. VISUALIZE SUCCESS. In the weeks leading up to the trail, I lost much sleep due to elaborate visualizations of what my new life would look like and how I would react. I envisioned myself going through the motions all the way to the point of summiting Mount Katahdin (the trail's northern terminus). This isn't voodoo or hocus-pocus. There is a lot of science to support the power of visualization. Mental repetitions are nearly as powerful as physical repetitions. Doing both is more important than doing either in isolation.

4. AVOID POST-TRAIL DEPRESSION. One of the most

rewarding aspects of thru-hiking the Appalachian Trail is pursuing a singular, monumental goal for the better part of a half year. It supplies a tremendous amount of purpose to one's life. Once you achieve said goal, it's as if a rug has been pulled from underneath you. I encourage all thru-hikers to have their next meaningful goal in mind by the time they finish.

COMEBACK LESSON: Having hiked through the emotional highs and lows of the Appalachian Trail, Zach chose to focus his advice on the mental fortitude that is necessary to achieve one's goals. Visualization was a key part of creating internal endurance, and rather than shying away from any possible problems, he mentally worked through them in elaborate visualizations. He also involved a cast of people around himself by making goals public, addressed deeply held emotions, and, to avoid post-trail depression, had the next goal in mind before even finishing. In other words, he'd thought things out way ahead of ever stepping foot on the 2,180-mile trail.

EAT LIKE A CHAMPION

You are what you eat. What would *you* like to be?
—JULIE MURPHY, AUTHOR

Chrissy Barth is passionate about teaching others optimal health and performance by taking the confusion out of nutrition. She is a registered dietitian, yoga teacher, and communications expert in the field of holistic nutrition. As founder and CEO of Nutrition.Lifestyle. Education—a nutrition coaching and consulting practice based in

Phoenix, Arizona—Chrissy serves as a consultant to sports teams (including the NFL's Arizona Cardinals), world-renowned spas, eating disorder programs, medical and training facilities, and corporations. She also serves as a spokesperson for local and national media outlets and is a lecturer at Arizona State University.

Chrissy shared with me five key suggestions for how endurance athletes can master their nutrition.

Many athletes don't take into account the significance nutrition plays in improving sports performance, enhancing recovery, decreasing injury, and reducing time lost to both injury and illness. Combining a high-quality sports diet and the timing of specific nutrients like carbohydrates and protein along with smart supplementation will result in a healthier athlete who will perform at his or her highest level.

In sports, where food is fuel, we sometimes forget that eating well is more than just bars and sports drinks. Let's do a quick calculation: If you get 8 hours of sleep a night, you're awake for 112 hours a week. A 20-hour-per-week training regimen leaves you with 92 nontraining hours. That's a good chunk of your waking life not spent eating gels and chugging down sports drinks. As an endurance machine, what you put in your mouth during those 92 hours can make the difference between functioning at your best and getting rusty—or, worse, hitting the wall.

Endurance sports tap into all systems of the body, and this is often done under extreme conditions, such as with high heat and humidity. Endurance athletes strive to be lean, agile, fast, and strong. The training regimen for most endurance athletes is a part-time time job and involves long workout sessions, usually including weight training, to help build and maintain lean body mass, and running, to optimize endurance.

The high-energy needs of endurance athletes require adequate protein to build and repair muscle tissue, carbohydrates for energy-restoring glycogen stores, and dietary fats for energy and endurance. Dietary fats are also crucial for absorbing specific nutrients—particularly the fat-soluble vitamins A, D, E, and K. Lastly, endurance athletes need to stay properly hydrated for optimal performance and to limit their risk of injury and illness. Here are the top-five nutrition musts for endurance athletes.

1. BUILD A HEALTHY FOUNDATION WITH THE "ATHLETE'S PLATE." Divide your plate into thirds with real food—fresh fruits and vegetables and healthy unsaturated fats, high-fiber starches, and proteins.

Choose fresh fruits and vegetables and the "good guy" unsaturated fats. Fruits and vegetables offer natural antioxidants and anti-inflammatories such as vitamins C and E and beta-carotene. The roles of these nutrients include lessening and preventing inflammation, optimizing the immune system, increasing energy levels, speeding up recovery, and decreasing the risk of disease. Aim to eat the rainbow: Get color on your plate from a variety of fruits and vegetables. The more color on your plate, the more vitamins and minerals for your body and brain. Choose healthy fats as your primary source of dietary fats. The best sources to reach for are nuts, seeds, vegetable and plant oils, vinaigrette-based salad dressings, natural peanut butter, avocados, trans fat–free margarine spreads, and cold-water fish such as salmon and tuna.

Choose carbohydrates that provide premium fuel for the body and brain. Eat more fiber-rich starches and fruits. High-fiber starches and fruits provide ample amounts of carbohydrates to help optimize energy levels. High-fiber starches include whole grains and starchy vegetables. Choose whole grains such as whole wheat pasta, whole grain breads, whole grain cereals, brown rice, quinoa, and wholewheat couscous. High-fiber starchy vegetables include potatoes, corn, peas, winter squash, and beans. These high-fiber starches, along with fruit, are excellent sources of complex carbohydrates, which will help fuel your training. Increase carbohydrates on active and practice days to top energy reserves. These carbohydrates are then stored as muscle glycogen for energy to be used later on. Limit quick or refined carbohydrates on less-active days. Refined carbohydrates—found in sweets, desserts, and soft drinks—will be stored as fat if not burned off.

Choose proteins to build and maintain muscle tissue and optimize the immune system. Aim for a variety of protein sources from either animal or plant origin. Proteins range from "lean" to "high-fat." Choose lean proteins the majority of the time. Lean proteins include chicken and turkey without the skin, 93 percent lean ground beef, buffalo or bison, sirloin, fish, eggs, low-fat dairy products, and nondairy alternatives such as soy milk, tofu, beans, and peanut butter. High-fat proteins, such as fried chicken, ribs, bacon, sausage, hot dogs, and full-fat dairy products, should be limited, as they are high in saturated fat, which contributes to heart disease. Choose higher-fat protein sources only on very active days and limit them on rest days, especially when taking a day or two off.

2. BREAKFAST IS FOR CHAMPIONS. Not only is breakfast one of the most important meals of the day, it could be your biggest mistake to skip, as breakfast accounts for 25 percent of your total energy needs for the day. Think about it—when was your last meal the previous night? If your last meal was at 7:00 p.m. and your first meal the next day isn't until noon, this results in 17 hours of fasting. When we skip meals, we start burning muscle. Also, missing out on the first meal of the day increases your risk of eating larger portions at night, when you are less active, promoting the storage of body fat and the potential for weight gain. Start the morning with a well-rounded breakfast as simple as a peanut butter and jelly sandwich on whole grain bread with a glass of low-fat milk.

3. DRINK FLUIDS EARLY AND OFTEN. Stay hydrated. We need approximately ½ to 1 ounce of fluid per pound of body weight. Less than that can lead to dehydration, which can hurt your performance and in extreme cases be life threatening. Don't wait until you're thirsty. By the time you feel thirst, you may be dehydrated. One way to monitor hydration is to keep an eye on the color of your urine. A pale yellow color means you're getting enough fluids. A dark color, like that of apple juice, means you're falling short. Because exercise causes rapid fluid loss, it's a good idea to drink fluids before as well as during training and events.

4. TIME YOUR NUTRIENTS FOR GREATER MUSCLE GAINS AND RECOVERY. Fuel within 15 to 30 minutes after your workout. Think of your muscles as a wet sponge postworkout; the longer you wait to refuel, the more that sponge is going to dry out, which makes it challenging for nutrients like carbohydrates to replenish what's been lost. This increases your risk of poor sports performance with a higher risk of getting injured. A ratio of 2–3 grams of carbohydrates per gram of protein has been proven to facilitate protein synthesis (muscle repair) and the refueling of glycogen (what you need in your body's gas tank). A 12-ounce glass of low-fat chocolate milk is one of the best postworkout recovery shakes.

5. EAT ENOUGH AND HAVE A HEALTHY RELATIONSHIP WITH FOOD. Food is fuel! Aim for three balanced meals and two to four snacks each day. In order to keep your body's gas tank full and maintain a high level of energy, eating every 3 to 4 hours will prevent your body from using muscle (protein) for energy and instead burn fat for fuel. Additional benefits include maintenance of blood sugar and lean muscle mass and the prevention of over-eating. Prepare and plan ahead; pack healthy snacks with you when you are on the go. These can include trail mix, sports bars, a peanut butter and jelly sandwich, or a small handful of almonds and a piece of fruit.

COMEBACK LESSON: Making a comeback by definition means that you're not currently at your peak performance state. An injury can put you on the sidelines, you may have taken some time away from the sport, or your game may have slowly regressed to a less than optimal form. In a similar way, our food habits can also change or have setbacks. For example, you became less careful about daily food habits after an injury, or you became accustomed to rich ample meals with more socializing during a period of time off, or your body began to require a different food focus as you got older. Take the comeback opportunity to reevaluate your current food patterns and habits, incorporate more optimal dietary inputs, and slowly but surely bring back a champion's meal plan. Food is fuel—upgrade to premium!

BEATING THE IRONMAN BLUES

I merely took the energy it takes to pout and wrote some blues.

—DUKE ELLINGTON, PIANIST, COMPOSER, AND BAND LEADER

Post-triathlon depression, commonly known as the "Ironman blues," is a very real phenomenon. Though we will discuss it mostly in the context of racing (relating to Ironman triathlons in particular), similar phenomena occur after all athletic competitions. The Ironman blues is just one version of postperformance blues: It can also happen after a major championship event, at the end of a long season, or after completing a marathon, cycling race, or even a major hike. When major competitions come to an end, athletes often have difficulty switching gears and transitioning back into a normal routine.

Psychologists have put forth several possible explanations for the Ironman blues. One explanation is called the "crisis of goal attainment." When we wake up in the morning, our goals set our agenda. When we achieve major goals, they no longer serve as organizing principles, and this often leaves us with a lack of focus and direction. Our agenda is no longer set. We often feel empty, wondering, "Now what?" or "What's next?"

The more a goal organizes our lives, the more its attainment can lead to crisis. Ironman competitions, in particular, demand that athletes devote immense resources (mental, physical, temporal, and financial) to training, which often leads to the neglect of other aspects of life, such as family, school, or work obligations. Athletes expend an extreme amount of physical, emotional, and mental energy, often over the course of many years, to prepare for an Ironman triathlon, but after the race they must return to everyday life.

A second, related explanation for the Ironman blues is that the short-term goals that can consume athletes before and during such competitions can easily distract them from major life issues, such as depression and anxiety, which would otherwise have to be acknowledged and addressed. But depression and anxiety often come back to the surface once the training-related distractions disappear. Sports can be a great distraction, but we can (and should) only ignore problems for so long. Eventually, we must face the music. And the longer we ignore our problems, the louder the music grows.

When Ironman athletes train and prepare for a race, they suspend other normal aspects of life, aspects that may be full of conflict. In this way, the narrow focus on training can be a "feel-good" exercise. Being able to call oneself an Ironman, in particular, can have an obvious effect on one's feelings of self-worth and self-esteem. But the ending of the race creates a void, and athletes are left asking, "Now what can I do that will make me feel good and valuable?" Athletes often answer this question by setting similarly lofty goals, from which they draw new feelings of self-worth and self-esteem while continuing to ignore other important aspects of life.

The third possible explanation for the Ironman blues is simple: After training subsides, athletes no longer experience the daily endorphin high caused by intense physical activity. The Ironman blues, according to this explanation, amounts to endorphin withdrawal.

Athletes who spend massive amounts of time, energy, and money preparing for major competitions, only to perform suboptimally, can also experience a form of postcompetition depression. This is quite common for perfectionists—even if they perform well, they will find a flaw and consider themselves failures. At some level, perfectionists never feel like they are good enough.

All athletes (all people, really) need to give themselves permission to be human. Humans are not perfect. One way to avoid such perfectionism is to realize that competitions may define what we do, but they do not define who we are. We can fail in a race without being failures. We never have to feel bad about ourselves if we have done our best. Our self-worth is *never* on the line in our athletic endeavors.

The best way to deal with the Ironman blues involves good preparation (forewarned is forearmed) and postrace debriefing. Meet with a sports psychologist to process your thoughts and feelings about your performance and outline a plan for the weeks and months that follow the race.

COMEBACK LESSON: Athletes should anticipate feeling somewhat lost for a period of time following a major competition. Understand that these feelings are normal. Now that we have discussed possible explanations for the Ironman blues, you have a better understanding of the causes of this uncomfortable phenomenon. This understanding alone can ameliorate the blues.

Athletes can set other goals, even if they are somewhat arbitrary, so that they have new organizing principles in their lives. But, as always, if one's blues require one to work through some unresolved or unacknowledged pain, then it may be important to explore this with a professional. Exploring such emotional pain is a very individual process that can help athletes beat the blues.

THE FINAL TAKEAWAY

Endurance and fitness challenges are as much mental as they are physical. While this is true for all athletic endeavors, endurance and fitness activities present unique and amplified mental challenges, such as possible intense discomfort for long periods of time. Fitness challenges take the body to physical limits that naturally extend to the mind. The body will be screaming at you to take a break, it will make your legs shake to warn you that things might be too much, and your heart will race as adrenaline courses through throbbing veins! In other words, your mind, thoughts, and emotions will be affected by training as much as your training will affect them.

All of these physical responses have to be met mentally in some way. This can include knowing what are your safe and optimal physical limits, applying pregame and preworkout mental routines to properly focus, and using your planning abilities to direct and nurture yourself through the extended period of training toward a peak competitive performance.

The mental side of the equation can be split into several sections. For example, there are techniques that you can apply during a match or race to stay in the zone, such as engaging in positive energetic self-talk and displaying confident and upbeat body language. In comparison, during practice, you can apply mental reminders about focus, reframe your perspective to make practice a reward rather than a punishment, and enlist supportive workout partners to keep each other going.

Lastly, over the long term, cognitive and higher-order mental planning and organization come into play and are vital, if not absolutely necessary, to incorporate training into a daily life that includes family, work, and social obligations. General coping mechanisms and ways to deal with stresses that come from outside your sport or training cannot be ignored if you are to put 100 percent into your game. In other words, at the end of the day, making a comeback is probably as much mental as it is physical!

CHAPTER SIX

AIR COMEBACK

If you're trying to achieve, there will be roadblocks.
I've had them; everybody has had them. But obstacles don't have to
stop you. If you run into a wall, don't turn around and give up.
Figure out how to climb it, go through it, or work around it.

—MICHAEL JORDAN

Michael Jeffrey Jordan was born in Brooklyn, New York, on February 17, 1963. He was the fourth of Deloris and James Jordan's five children. Growing up in Wilmington, North Carolina, Michael excelled in sports from an early age, often motivated by his desire to outdo his older brother Larry.

As you probably know, Jordan went on to become an elite athlete, arguably the best the sport of basketball has ever seen. ESPN rated him as the top North American athlete of the 20th century. A global icon, his story plays out as a journey through struggles and setbacks to the comebacks that led him to multiple championships. Millions wanted to "be like Mike," but for Jordan himself, being like Mike took hard work; it was not predestined or guaranteed.

Jordan's first major setback came when he was cut from the Laney High School varsity basketball team during his sophomore year.

Jordan responded by wiping away his tears and working diligently on his game. He also happened to grow 4 inches the following summer. He felt he had something to prove, both to himself and to others, and he did so by making the varsity team as a junior. Not only that, he averaged 25 points per game. This was his first comeback.

Jordan continued to work on his game, so much so that he averaged a triple-double during his senior year: 29.2 points, 11.6 rebounds, and 10.1 assists. People from near and far made their way to see him play, and there was rarely an empty seat in the house. He was selected as a McDonald's All-American, among other honors. Not only did he dazzle on the basketball court, but he also starred on Laney's varsity baseball team.

Jordan accepted a scholarship to play basketball at the University of North Carolina at Chapel Hill. He quickly became a star under the tutelage of head coach Dean Smith. During his freshman year, Jordan drained what has become an iconic shot to help UNC defeat Georgetown University in the 1982 NCAA Championship game. Following his junior year in 1984, Jordan was awarded the Naismith Trophy as player of the year and named to the Wooden Award All-American Team.

Instead of coming back for his senior year, Jordan declared himself eligible for the 1984 NBA draft. He was selected by the Chicago Bulls with the No. 3 overall pick. During his rookie season, he led the Bulls to the playoffs for the first time since 1981, averaging 28.2 points per game during the regular season. He was selected as an NBA All-Star and named Rookie of the Year.

Jordan was sidelined for most of the next season by a broken foot, missing 64 games. Coming back for the 1986–87 season, he torched the league, averaging an astonishing 37.1 points per game to win the first of his 10 scoring titles. Famed for his clutch shots, highlight-reel dunks, and tenacious defense, "Air Jordan" was on the fast track to becoming the most incredible athlete in the world.

Despite MJ's individual greatness, the Bulls suffered numerous playoff setbacks and disappointments on their quest to win their first NBA championship. The Detroit Pistons, known as the Bad Boys for their aggressive style (dirty, according to some), bounced the Bulls out of the playoffs in three straight seasons (1988–1990), serving as the biggest and most pertinent obstacle to the Bulls' championship hopes. The Pistons won NBA titles in 2 out of these 3 years—1989 and 1990.

It's not often remembered now, but many in the media said Jordan was just a scorer, and that this didn't help his team win. It was also thought that having a player like that at the shooting guard position wasn't ideal. Basically, the narrative at the time was that Jordan could score and score, but all that amounted to was scoring titles and personal stats, not a better team and not championships.

The Bulls' big breakthrough came in the 1990–91 season, when they finished first in the NBA's Central Division with a 61–21 record. After thumping the New York Knicks and the Philadelphia 76ers in the first two rounds of the playoffs, Chicago faced Detroit, their mighty foe, in the Eastern Conference finals. This time, the Bulls swept the Pistons in four games. They then went on to defeat the Los Angeles Lakers in five games to win their first NBA title.

The Bulls won their second straight title in 1992, overcoming the Portland Trail Blazers in six games. During the 1992 Summer Olympics in Barcelona, Jordan won his second Olympic gold medal as a member of America's "Dream Team" (he had won his first gold medal at the 1984 Los Angeles games).

In 1993, the Bulls won their third consecutive title, defeating the Phoenix Suns in six games. The Bulls had completed what has come to be known as a "three-peat," one of the most difficult feats in professional sports. Jordan was selected as the NBA finals Most Valuable Player each year.

After a tragic carjacking in which his father was killed, Jordan shocked the sports world by retiring from basketball at the age of 30. He was at the pinnacle of his profession, but he had lost motivation. He turned to a game he first played with his father, taking a swing at professional baseball. Jordan, the most famous athlete in the world, paid his dues with the Birmingham Barons, a minor-league affiliate of the Chicago White Sox. Despite the hard work, it appeared unlikely he would be called to join the White Sox. Whether he was looking for motivation to come back to basketball or not, he found it.

In 1995, Jordan announced his return to the NBA in Terminator-esque style and simplicity, releasing a one-line statement through his agent: "I'm back." Once again, Jordan would go on to lead the Bulls to three consecutive NBA championships. The Bulls won their sixth Jordan-led championship against the Utah Jazz, with MJ knocking down a go-ahead 20-footer with 5.2 seconds left in Game 6. What a glorious comeback!

Jordan would retire for a second time, during the 1998–99 season, making January 13, 1999, his last day as a Chicago Bull. Despite his retirement, Jordan's love of basketball and competitive fire still burned brightly. In 2001, he decided to play again, this time as a member of the Washington Wizards. His first season back, he led the team in scoring, assists, and steals. He also donated his entire salary that year to the recovery effort and victims' families of 9/11. In 2002–03, he played all 82 games and averaged 20 points per game, before retiring for the third and final time.

Jordan ended his Hall of Fame career with six NBA championship rings, six NBA finals MVPs, and the record for most career points per game with a 30.12 average. He led the 1995–96 Bulls to a 72–10 record, establishing a still-standing NBA single-season record. As the best player on the planet, he remained dedicated to continuous improvement. As such, Jordan epitomized the famous Zen saying "When you get to the top of the mountain, keep climbing."

MJ'S HALL OF FAME INDUCTION SPEECH

Never say never, because limits, like fears, are often just an illusion.

—MICHAEL JORDAN

Michael Jordan was a first-ballot selection to the Naismith Memorial Basketball Hall of Fame in Springfield, Massachusetts, as part of the class of 2009. Also included in Jordan's induction class were San Antonio Spurs center David Robinson, Utah Jazz point guard John Stockton, Utah Jazz coach Jerry Sloan, and Rutgers University women's coach C. Vivian Stringer.

In his acceptance speech, Jordan very clearly describes his family's competitive nature and his mother's strength. He thanks them for passing those characteristics on to him. He took their competitive nature and worked hard. Beyond this, he speaks about times when he sought out the help of others and other times when he faced obstacles that might limit his potential or place a ceiling on his achievements. These stories teach us about the level of hard work, mental preparation, self-examination, and consistent effort it took to maintain his skills and competitive edge on the world's biggest stage, against the world's best competition.

The comeback principles discussed throughout the book show themselves in Jordan's induction speech.

LET GO—release the mental brick

LOOK FOR SUPPORT—build a winning team

LOVE THE GAME—compete with purpose and passion

LEARN—embrace a growth mind-set

LABOR—keep pounding the rock

LEARN OPTIMISM—believe in your comeback story

LEAN ON YOUR MENTAL GAME—win the game from within yourself

A partial transcript of Jordan's speech is provided below. Each of the Champion's Comeback Code strategies is discussed. Several of these strategies can be seen in each part of the speech:

Look for Support: Build a Winning Team

Thank you. I told all my friends I was just gonna come up here and say "Thank you" and walk off. I can't. There's no way. I got so many people I gotta thank. In all the videos, you never just saw me; you saw Scottie Pippen. Every championship I won. I've had a lot of questions over the last 4 weeks, and everybody's saying, well, "Why'd you pick David Thompson?" I know why, and David knows why, and maybe you guys don't know why, but as I grew up in North Carolina, I was 11 years old in 1974, I think, when you guys won the championship. . . .

I was in love with David Thompson. Not just for the game of basketball, but in terms of what he represented. You know, we all—as Vivian said—we go through our trials and tribulations. And, he did. And I was inspired by him. . . . [When I asked him to introduce me,] he was very kind and said, "Yeah, I'll do it." And that wasn't out of disrespect to any of my Carolina guys, they all know I'm a true blue Carolina guy to the heart. Coach [Dean] Smith, Larry Brown, Sam Perkins, James Worthy—you know, all of those guys.

MJ picked former NBA player David Thompson to introduce him at his Hall of Fame enshrinement ceremony. The point here is that our support system can include more than the most obvious members of our "team." Jordan mentions all of the obvious Carolina guys, but Thompson provided an important source of inspiration. We won't all be lucky enough to have someone like Thompson on our team, but we can have a lot of Thompson-like people if we look in unexpected places for inspiration, guidance, and support. So who is your own David Thompson?

Love the Game: Compete with Purpose and Passion

Well it all starts with my parents. You guys see all the highlights; what is it about me that you guys don't know? . . . I got two brothers, James and Larry, they're 5'4", 5'5" in height. They gave me all I could ever ask for as a brother in terms of competition. . . . [Larry] fought me every single day. And to the extent that my mother used to come out and make us come in because we were fighting way too much. And my older brother was always gone—he served in the army for 31 years.

And the competition didn't stop there. My sister, who is 1 year younger than me, Roz, never wanted to be home by herself. She took classes—extra classes—to graduate from high school with *me*, to go to University of North Carolina with *me,* and to graduate prior to *me.* And you guys sit there asking where is my competition or where did my competitive nature come from? It came from them. It came from my older sister, who's not here today. And my father, who's not here today—obviously he's with us in all of us. I mean, my competitive nature has gone a long way from the first time I picked up any sport: Baseball, football, ran track, basketball; anything to miss class, I played it.

So they started the fire in me. That fire started with my parents. And as I moved on in my career, people added wood to that fire.

Where then do you find your unique passion? Who provides you with the kindling, the space, and the support for the fire that once lit becomes over time your personal passion? The passion MJ is talking about here seems to be a love of competition, as well as a love of and for his family. A love of competition, fueled by loved ones, turned into love for the game of basketball.

Let Go: Release the Mental Brick

Coach [Dean] Smith, you know, what else can I say about him? You know, he's legendary in the game of coaching. And then there's Leroy Smith. Now you guys think that's a myth. Leroy Smith was a guy when I got cut he made the team—on the varsity team—and he's here tonight. He's still the same 6'7" guy. He's not any bigger, probably his game is about the same. But he started the whole process with me, because when he made the team and I didn't, I wanted to prove not just to Leroy Smith, not just to myself, but to the coach who actually picked Leroy over me, I wanted to make sure you understood you made a mistake, dude.

And then there's Buzz Peterson, my roommate. Now when I first met Buzz, all I heard about was this kid from Asheville, North Carolina, who is Player of the Year. I'm thinking, "Well he ain't never played against me yet, so how did he become Player of the Year?" Is that some type of media exposure? You know I came from Wilmington; you know we had two channels, channel ABC and channel NBC, and that was it. I never saw NBA sports at all when I grew up; we didn't have CBS affiliation in North Carolina, in Wilmington, so Buzz Peterson became a dot on my board. And when I got the chance to meet Buzz Peterson on the basketball court or in person, Buzz was a great person, it wasn't a fault of his. It was just that my competitive nature—I didn't think that he could beat me, or that he was better than me as a basketball player. And he became my roommate. And from that point on, he became a focal point—not knowingly; he didn't know it—but he did.

And Coach Smith, the day that he was on the *Sports Illustrated* [cover] and he named four starters and he didn't name me, that burned me up, because I thought I belonged on that *Sports Illustrated*. Now he had his own vision about giving a freshman that exposure, and I totally understand that, but from a basketball sense, I deserved to be on that *Sports Illustrated*, and he understands that.

Sometimes getting better doesn't just "appear" from noble aspirations. Sometimes it comes from hurts, slights, and failures. These are important because they force us to dig deeper. Those who tend to misinterpret MJ's speech as being egotistical don't realize this truth. Nobody starts out as Michael Jordan. He used to just be a tall skinny kid who tried to make his high school basketball team.

There are few, if any, champions who reach their special pinnacle on their own. I think the critics of this speech don't understand that point. Jordan is not disparaging others. He is recognizing them as competitors, critics, and supporters alike. Jordan believes they all added value to his quest to become a champion, and that value is important to success because it provides added motivation.

In terms of grudges, Jordan didn't seem to do much letting go. He carried these mental bricks around with him, but they didn't seem to weigh him down. He took these bricks and trained with them strapped to his back so that when he competed, he was light as air. Leroy Smith wasn't the only guy who beat Jordan to make varsity. Every single player on the roster did. Jordan needed to focus his energies on slights or certain people. He channeled this and it worked for him.

It's hard to let go. And sometimes carrying a little baggage with us can make us better prepared for our journey. It's hard to know when to let go and when to make a Buzz Peterson dartboard. But it's something we should think about as we look inside and try to figure out how to be our best.

Lean on Your Mental Game: Win the Game from within Yourself

And it didn't stop there. You know, my competitive nature went right into the pros; I get to the Bulls, which I was very proud [of]. . . . Kevin Loughery was my first coach. Kevin used to take practices and put me in the starting five, and he'd make it a competitive thing where the losing team would have to run. So now I'm on the winning team, and halfway in the game, halfway in the situations, he would switch me to the losing team.

So I take that as a competitive thing of you trying to test me, and 9 times out of 10 the second team would come back and win no matter what he did. So I appreciate Kevin Loughery for giving me that challenge—you know, providing that type of fire within me; he threw another log on that fire for me.

Coach Loughery knew that the best competition for MJ was MJ himself. So he'd have Jordan run up the score for one team in one half and then have him play from behind with the other team the next half. So Jordan was put into situations where he'd have to play from behind, something he might not otherwise have had to do in practice but that he'd eventually face in games. MJ had to keep *laboring,* because once he'd worked hard to build a lead for his team, he suddenly found himself with that lead to overcome on the other team. He had to *learn optimism.* It's easy to feel dejected when put in that position. Being in these situations helped him learn and grow. He could have gotten upset and not embraced the opportunity, but he used it as a learning and growing opportunity.

It's always easy to be on the winning team, but what about being on the losing team? What do you do then? How do you come back? How do you help the team and yourself be more successful? Or if you are already successful on that team, how do you contribute to make others as successful and thus benefit yourself? When the odds are stacked against you, what are you made of? Champions always find out.

Learn Optimism: Believe in Your Comeback Story

Jerry Reinsdorf [Bulls owner], I mean, what else can I say? The next year I came back, I broke my foot, and I was out for 65 games. And when I came back, I wanted to play; you know, he and the doctors came up with this whole theory that you can only play 7 minutes a game, but I'm practicing 2 hours a day. I'm saying, "Well, I don't think—I don't agree with that math, you know?" And back then it was about whoever had the worst record got the most balls and the Ping-Pong balls and you know you can decide what [draft] pick you're gonna have, but I didn't care about that, I just wanted to win. I wanted to make the playoffs. I wanted to keep that energy going in Chicago. So I had to go in his office and sit down with him and say, "Jerry, you know I feel like I should play more than 14 minutes, I've been practicing 2 hours." And he said, "MJ, I think I have to protect the long-term investment that we've invested in you." And I said, "Jerry, I really think I should be able to play." And he said, "Let me ask you this: If you had a headache—" And you know, at that time it was about a 10 percent chance that I could reinjure my ankle or my foot. And he said, "If you had a headache and you got 10 tablets and one of them is coated with cyanide, would you take the [tablet]?" And I looked at him and I said, "How bad is the headache? Depends on how bad the headache is." Jerry looked at me and he said, "Yeah, okay, I guess that's a good answer; you can go back and play." And he let me go back and play.

You know, Jerry provided a lot of different obstacles for me, but at the same time the guy gave me an opportunity to perform at the highest level in terms of basketball. And the Bulls—the whole Bulls organization did a great justice for me and for all of my teammates. Believe me, I had a lot of teammates over the 14 years that I played for the Bulls. You know I respected each and every one of them, I just wanted to win.

MJ obviously believed in himself. He went into Reinsdorf's office every day and tried to force that optimism on him. It may or may not have been smart. He could have reinjured himself—it's happened to others. But it took a lot of *optimism* either way.

Jordan was not concerned about the Bulls getting a better draft pick. If he was good enough to play, he wanted to play. He loved to play (*Love the game—compete with purpose and passion*).

Playing is just what he wanted to keep doing. He didn't want it easier on himself or the team by getting a higher pick. He worked hard to recover from injury, and now he wanted to work hard in games (*Labor—keep pounding the rock*).

Love the Game: Compete with Purpose and Passion

Then along came Doug Collins who was caught in the whole midst of this [Bulls general manager] Jerry Krause and Jerry Reinsdorf. And, at the same time, you know when I was trying to play in the summertime, he said, "Well, you're a part of the organization, and the organization said you can't play in the summertime." And I said, "Doug, you haven't read the fine print in my contract. In my contract, I have the 'love the game clause' that means I can play anytime I want, anyplace I want." And Doug looked at me and said, "Yeah, you're right, you're right." And that's how we became a little closer, in terms of Doug Collins and myself.

"Love of the game is in my contract," said Jordan. He wanted to practice and play on his own during the off-season whenever he had the opportunity. He loved to *work* over the summer (*Labor— keep pounding the rock*). It wasn't just play.

Is there a "love of the game clause" in your life contract? What does having this love mean to you? In terms of winning or contributing? Playing hard when losing? Playing with rules and abiding by them to be a better, more honorable player?

Look for Support: Build a Winning Team

My mom, what else can I say about my mom? My mom never stays still. You think I'm busy? She's always on the go. And without her—she's a rock, she's unbelievable. Right now she takes over two jobs. She's an unbelievable woman. If I've got anybody that's nagging me each and every day, it is her. And she constantly keeps me focused on the good things about life—you know, how people perceive you, how you respect them, you know, what's good for the kids, what's good for you. How you are perceived publicly; take a pause and think about the things that you do. And that all came from my parents, you know it came from my mom. And she's still at this stage—I'm 46 years old—she's still parenting me today. And that's the good thing about that lady, I love her to death. I love her to death.

Here MJ acknowledges his mom as his greatest support. She helps him to stay focused on the "good things about life" (*Learn optimism— believe in your comeback story*). There are several sources of support that you can seek out and appreciate, from your mother and father to a teacher or a coach or a fellow player or even a close friend who isn't in sports, even a spouse or significant other. Recognize their support and keep it and use it positively on the road to becoming a champion. Say "thank you" more often and encourage them, too.

Labor: Keep Pounding the Rock

And I'm going to thank a couple people that you guys probably wouldn't even think that I would thank. Isiah Thomas, Magic Johnson, George Gervin—now they say it was a so-called freeze-out in my rookie season. I wouldn't have ever guessed, but you guys gave me the motivation to say, "You know what, evidently I haven't proved enough to these guys. I gotta prove to them that I deserve what I've gotten on this level." And no matter what people may have said (if it was a rumor, I never took it as truth), but you guys never froze me out, because I was just happy to be there, no matter how you look at it. And from that point forward I wanted to prove to you—Magic, Larry [Bird], George, everybody—that I deserved to be on this level as much as everybody else. And hopefully over the period of my career I've done that, without a doubt, you know even in the Detroit years, we've done that.

Pat Riley, I mean, you and I, we go way back. I still remember in Hawaii—you remember in Hawaii, you and I—I was coming in and you were, I guess, leaving and you decided to stay a couple extra days, but you were in my suite. And they came and they told you you had to get out of my suite. And you slid a note underneath my door—although you had to move; you did move—you slid a note, saying, "I enjoyed the competition, congratulations. But we will meet again." And I take the heart in that because I think in all honesty you're just as competitive as I am, even from a coaching standpoint. And you challenged me every time I played the Knicks, the Heat—and I don't think you were with the Lakers—but anytime I played against you, you had "Jordan stoppers" on your team; you had John Starks, who I loved. You even had my friend Charles Oakley saying, "We can't go to lunch, we can't go to dinner, because Pat doesn't believe in fraternizing between the two of us." And this guy hit me harder than anybody else in the league, and he was my best friend. Patrick Ewing—we had the same agent, we came at the same time, but we couldn't go to lunch. Why is this? You think

I'm gonna play against Patrick any different than I play against anybody else? No, no.

And then you had your little guy, who was on your staff, who became the next coach after you: Jeff Van Gundy. He said I conned the players, I befriended them, and then I attacked them on the basketball court. Where did that come from? I just so happen to be a friendly guy. I get along with everybody, but at the same time when the light comes on, I'm just as competitive as anybody you know. So you guys, I have to say thank you very much for that motivation that I desperately needed.

Don't back down when playing in your own game and your own life! Jordan kept working hard, didn't back down to gamesmanship or intimidation, and was thus able to find success faster.

Learn: Embrace a Growth Mind-Set

Phil Jackson. Phil Jackson to me, he's a professional Dean Smith. He challenged me mentally, not just physically. You know, he understood the game, along with Tex Winter. They taught me a lot about the basketball game, Tex being the specialist; you know I could never please Tex. And I love Tex. Tex is not here, but I know he's here in spirit. I can remember a game coming off the basketball court, and we were down, I don't know 5–10 points, and I go off for about 25 points and we come back and win the game. And we're walking off the floor and Tex looks at me and says, "You know, there's no I in team." And I said, "Tex, there's not, there's not an I in team, but there's an I in win." I think he got my message: I'll do anything to win. You know, if that means we play team format, we win. If that means I have to do whatever I have to do, we gonna win no matter how you look at it.

MJ was eager to improve and demonstrated a willingness to learn from his coaches, including Phil Jackson, Dean Smith, and Tex Winter. "My best skill was that I was coachable. I was a sponge and aggressive to learn," said Jordan.

He also knew when to spell *team* and when to spell *win*. That knowledge is learned, and it requires one to have a strong mind-set (*Lean on your mental game—win the game from within yourself*). And it also requires the self-confidence to trust your training and your talent.

Lean on Your Mental Game: Win the Game from within Yourself

And then you had all your media naysayers. Oh, "Scoring champion can't win an NBA title." Or "You're not as good as Magic Johnson, you're not as good as Larry Bird. You're good, but you're not as good as those guys." You know, I had to listen to all of this, and that put so much wood on that fire that it kept me, each and every day, trying to get better as a basketball player. Now I'm not saying that they were wrong; I may have looked at it from a different perspective. But at the same time, as a basketball player I'm trying to become the best that I can, you know, and for someone like me who achieved a lot over the time of my career, you look for any kind of messages that people may say or do to get you motivated to play the game of basketball at the highest level, because that is when I feel like I excel at my best.

MJ didn't let any of the naysayers drag him down. This obviously takes *optimism* (*Learn optimism—believe in your comeback story*). More than that, it takes a really strong belief in oneself. Jordan certainly had that.

Jordan turned all the "hater-ade" into fuel for his own competitive fire. Deal with naysayers in your own game and life by ignoring them or using what they say for extra motivation. Find what you are the best at and work toward accomplishing it despite the critics.

Learn Optimism: Believe in Your Comeback Story

And the last one that you guys have probably seen—I hate to do it to him, but he's such a nice guy. When I first met Bryon Russell . . . I was in Chicago in 1994. I was working out for baseball, and they came down for a workout and shootaround and I came over to say hello. And at this time, I had no thoughts of coming back and playing the game of basketball, and Bryon Russell came over to me and said, "You know what, man, why'd you quit? Why'd you quit? You know I could guard you. If I ever see you in a pair of shorts. If I ever see you in a pair of shorts."

So when I did decide to come back in 1995, and then we played Utah in '96, I'm at the Center Circle and

Bryon Russell is sitting next to me, and I look over to Bryon and I said, "Do you remember this conversation you made in 1994, or when you 'I think I can guard you, I can shut you down, and I would love to play against you.' Well, you are about to get your chance." And believe me, ever since that day, he got his chance. I don't know how successful he was, but I think he had his chance, and believe me I relished on that point, and from this day forward if I ever see him in shorts, I'm coming at him.

MJ received a bit of competitive ribbing from Utah Jazz guard Bryon Russell, who came upon Jordan after his first retirement and told him, "I think I can guard you, I can shut you down." Later, when Jordan returned to basketball, he decided to goad Russell a bit by saying, "Well, now you have your chance." In actuality, that comment was MJ giving himself a chance to excel once more. It was Russell whom Jordan beat for his game-winning shot in Game 6 of the 1998 NBA finals. Take this example and turn it into a personal mantra: Excel or re-excel when people don't think you can!

Love the Game: Compete with Purpose and Passion

The game of basketball has been everything to me. My refuge. My place I've always gone when I needed to find comfort and peace. It's been a source of intense pain, and a source of most intense feelings of joy and satisfaction.

And one that no one can even imagine. It's been a relationship that has evolved over time and has given me the greatest respect and love for the game. It has provided me with a platform to share my passion with millions in a way I neither expected nor could have imagined in my career. I hope that it's given the millions of people that I've touched the optimism and the desire to achieve their goals through hard work, perseverance, and positive attitude.

Although I'm recognized with this tremendous honor of being in the Basketball Hall of Fame, I don't look at this moment as a defining end to my relationship with the game of basketball. It's simply a continuation of something that I started a long time ago. One day you might look up and see me playing the game at 50. Oh, don't laugh. Never say never. Because limits, like fears, are often just an illusion. Thank you very much. I look forward to it.

Here Jordan explains why sports and growth are important to him and to many other people as well. Heralded by many as the greatest basketball player of all time, and at a point where many people would be winding down, Jordan continues to apply his principles, saying, "One day you might look up and see me playing the game at 50. Oh, don't laugh," Jordan added as he closed his speech. If you laugh, he's likely to take that laugh as a challenge and do it!

Jordan's comments here relate to both his persistence and his love of the game. The love of what you do, a love so strong that you will keep on doing it for all of your life even after you become a champion, and especially after you retire or have gotten older, must always remain. It is always better to set no limits and have the limitations wide open to learning more and achieving even more than you thought you were ever capable of.

THE FINAL TAKEAWAY

While Michael Jordan was a stellar athlete, and a champion's champion, he was human, just like the rest of us. That means that he had plenty to overcome on his way to the top. It also means, as we saw, that he wasn't always the perfect embodiment of the 7 L's. While his life gives us many examples of *love, learn,* and *labor,* it's clear that his greatest difficulty was *letting go.* But he always used the negativity to his advantage.

Your comeback story may also highlight some of the 7 L's more than others. That's okay. Keep them all in mind and be ready to draw on them when you need to. Don't feel pressure to put them all into play right away. Applying the Champion's Comeback Code strategies should never end for you, your goals, and in your drive toward success and becoming a champion at whatever you love to do.

CHAPTER SEVEN

THE CHAMPION'S MENTAL SUCCESS ACADEMY

When you clearly envision the outcome of victory, engrave it upon your heart, and are firmly convinced that you will attain it, your brain makes every effort to realize the mental image you have created. And then, through your unceasing efforts, that victory is finally made a reality.

—DAISAKU IKEDA, PHILOSOPHER

How do athletes gain the confidence they need to make a major comeback or forge ahead and go where they have never gone before—win a big event, ace an important fitness test, or come through in the clutch for the first time? How do they come to believe they can win at the highest level without any prior experience or any point of reference to encourage them? Stepping up under pressure is never easy, but all successful competitors must undertake this progression and seize their best moments by first seeing and feeling themselves victorious and by preparing themselves to be victorious.

This chapter offers eight specific scripts to guide you through powerful sessions of visualization. These scripts are related to both comebacks and succeeding the first time by overcoming the odds. You will learn how to get mentally psyched for competition, rebound when you've just failed, or overcome an injury and the fear of reinjury. You can practice visualization on your own and develop the ability to hone the key skills and strategies you need to reach your next level of performance.

When 18-year-old Mikaela Shiffrin won the gold medal at the 2014 Sochi games, she became the youngest slalom champion in Olympic alpine skiing history. As she explained to reporters, prior to the competition she made extensive use of visualization to prepare herself for the games. "I've been here before in my head for sure. To everybody this is my first Olympics, but to me it's my thousandth."

The body reacts to the mental pictures we form. For example, think about giving a speech in front of a huge auditorium full of people. Imagine that, even with your family and friends there, your fellow students or colleagues are ready make fun of you or crack jokes and post your flubs online at the press of a button. As you think about this, your palms sweat, your pulse races, and your legs get wobbly—but you're still at home just thinking about this!

The mental world can be very real.

Champions use visualization as mental training. Grete Waitz, nine-time winner of the New York City Marathon, said, "Spend at least some of your training time, and other parts of your day, concentrating on what you are doing in training and visualizing your success."

Thinking about an upcoming situation can get your heart pounding. Close your eyes, or keep them slightly open with a soft focus. Use your mind's ability to see mental images to your advantage by visualizing a positive performance. This is just as powerful as physical training. Picture the ideal steps for achieving a success-ful result—the more details the better. Create a crystal clear, posi-tive mental image and let the emotional and physical feelings surrounding this successful moment emerge.

Let your mind be the prelude to your feelings. Include the sights (vivid colors), noises (stereo sound), smells, textures, and powerful emotions that accompany your performance. Moving your body to mimic performance during this rehearsal can also be helpful. The clarity and controllability of your images will improve with practice.

Hall of Fame pitcher John Smoltz played 21 seasons, earned eight All-Star selections, and won the World Series with the 1995 Atlanta Braves. The following year, he won the National League Cy Young Award. He knew the power of visualization. "I envi-sioned I pitched 100 Game 7s when I was a kid. I put myself in every scenario you could imagine. I allowed myself in my imagina-tion to win it in every one of those," said Smoltz.

Alpine ski racer Lindsey Vonn has won four overall World Cup titles and the gold medal in downhill at the 2010 Winter Olympics in Vancouver. She uses visualization to stay sharp while recovering from injuries and always visualizes her run before she races. "By the time I get to the start gate, I've run that race 100 times already in my head, picturing how I'll take the turns."

If you really want to succeed at a particular move or skill, visual-ize yourself doing it properly and powerfully over and over again. Give it a try right now: Select a specific skill in your sport, such as taking a penalty kick in soccer, hammering the hills on a cross-country course, exploding from the starting blocks on the track, or taking your lead to prepare to steal second base. Begin by creating a mental picture of your environment, progressively including all of the sights and sounds that you can think of. Think about preparing to take à free throw in basketball or make a serve in tennis. When you are spinning or bouncing a ball, can you see the seams?

Challenge yourself to do this exercise successfully three times in a row with full focus and a positive result. Remember that you are laying down "traction," which consists of mental grooves that are like the muscle memory you build with physical practice and repetition. If you miss the shot, stumble out of the blocks, or lose focus, keep repeating the process until you can visualize yourself doing it right—straight through to the goal.

- Spend 10 to 15 minutes every other day envisioning yourself refining your technique, playing at the peak of your abilities, managing missteps, coming through in the clutch, and accomplishing your goals.

- Use all of your senses and be sure to fill in all of the details— see and feel the desired result and the ideal steps for achieving it.

- Perform a mental dry run of your next competition or a specific game scenario. Mentally play out what you want to happen. The clearer you imagine your performance, the greater the likelihood that the reality will match your imagination.

Visualization is a type of mental practice that takes place inside the mind instead of in the arena, boardroom, or classroom. When visualizing, one starts by imagining and accepting all the sensations and emotions of a competition—the smell of the freshly mown grass, the touch of the wind in the trees and the sun or rain, the deafening crowd noise or silence, and the butterflies (that feel more like bees or hornets).

The competitor who uses visualization successfully takes that process as earnestly as any other aspect of preparation. It takes concentration and effort. Distractions are not allowed while going through visualization routines—making the experience so vivid that *only victory* happens, which is the opposite of daydreaming, during which *anything* can happen.

Of course, achieving success in all pursuits requires much more than a vivid imagination. Physical skills, as well as technical and tactical expertise, must be polished through real-world practice. But visualization can facilitate the learning process. Beyond this, it can help enhance the mental qualities required of great competitors: confidence, focus, emotional control, and motivation.

YOUR OWN CHAMPION'S MIND SCRIPTS

To practice mentally and hone mental skills and strategies needed to reach the next level of performance, I've created these visualization scripts to guide today's busy performers through powerful visualization sessions. You can read these visualization exercises anytime and anywhere. Read them at night before going to sleep, read them during any downtime you have in your day, or read them on the road while traveling to an event or competition. Read (or listen to) them enough times until the scenes are etched in your neurons.

Start practicing now by selecting the scripts you are most interested in from the eight listed below. Remember, daydreaming treats triumph and disaster the same, while visualization is only about triumph. Visualization takes focus and attention. Like practice sessions in all sports or study sessions in all classes, what you put into visualization will equal what you get from it. Champion yourself in all areas of life.

1. Sports Visualization Exercise

2. Comeback Visualization Exercise

3. Marathon Visualization Exercise

4. Swimming Visualization Exercise

5. Academics Visualization Exercise

6. Workplace Visualization Exercise

7. Fitness Visualization Exercise

8. Injury-Recovery Visualization Exercise

Sports Visualization Exercise

PART 1

Lie down in bed or, if you prefer, sit comfortably with your back straight. In your mind's eye, see yourself *in the moment*—sitting on a comfortable armchair inside a dimly lit private movie theater. In front of you is a large sky blue screen that will play a video of one of your sports performances.

Imagine that you're preparing for a competition. Think about the details of the competition.

• What kind of competition is this?

• Where is the competition?

• How will it look?

• Who will be in the stands?

• Who will be your opponent?

• What do you want to accomplish with this mental rehearsal?

Next, begin to see the scenes play themselves out on the screen, like a movie, and watch the competition play itself out. Watch the video. See yourself warming up properly and preparing to perform. Absorb the energy and excitement of competition. Soon it will be time to compete!

Now, turn your attention to the correct execution of the techniques or skills associated with your sport. Watch yourself performing solidly for a few moments. Notice the full focus that you have while competing. Then give yourself some challenging scenarios. See yourself make a mistake or respond to something that goes wrong. Then notice yourself making the proper adjustments to help you get back on the right track. Just trust yourself, love your game, and enjoy your feelings. Good job!

Next, look around and see your teammates (if you play a team sport) encouraging you, and know that you support them, too. For individual-sport athletes, look around and see friends and fans supporting you. Take in your surroundings and feel the energy. Continue to feel centered and in the zone. Visualize some additional successful moments in the competition.

In a couple of moments, the video will end. Tie up loose ends. Okay, good job. We are now at the end of the first run-through of the video. Continue to imagine yourself in your private movie theater, sitting in the comfortable armchair.

PART 2

Now, in the second part of this mental exercise, instead of watching yourself on-screen, place yourself in the video and see yourself as if you are in the scenes. The only difference from Part 1 is that you are now "inside" the video.

Take your mind there now. Step into the video and begin your precompetition routine. That's right. Notice your surroundings, whether they are sights, sounds, or people. As you visualize your surroundings, feel that you are looking through your own eyes, listening through your own ears, and feeling the movement in your own body. You can even feel the fabric of your clothes against your skin.

As in Part 1, the competition begins. Feel the fun and enjoyment of competing. Focus on what you are doing. You can feel a sense of confidence and control while fully executing your skills and techniques.

As earlier, you soon encounter a challenge yet notice that you are ready to adapt and respond. See yourself and know that you are easily able to correct any mistakes and make the adjustments necessary to get back on the right track.

In this moment, you are in complete control of your body, your state of mind, and your overall performance.

Visualize yourself going through a few more challenging scenarios. See, feel, and trust your training and your talent. Accept this truth: The better the competition, the more you are challenged and the more enjoyable the experience.

After moving through your challenges, return to a typical competitive scenario, taking it on fluidly and without hesitation. Take a moment to notice everything around you.

• Your teammates are engaged in their roles or perhaps cheering you on.

• You feel connected to them and are supporting them as well.

• You can feed off or tune out the fans as needed.

• You feel that your body is strong, full of energy, and you are mentally in the zone.

Run through a few more competitive scenarios as the video nears its conclusion. Feel the motion and pace of the competition. Let your body and intuition take over. Good job. You are now at the end of the video.

Now prepare to step back into the viewing room and sit in your comfortable armchair. Take this opportunity to reflect on what you visualized, on what was good about your game or performance.

- What went well?

- What were your highlights?

- What adjustments did you make in response to challenges?

- How did you feel when you were at your best?

In the future, remember this feeling. After quiet reflection, start to feel yourself in your bed or chair. Feel yourself come back to your current surroundings. Focus your attention on your feet; wiggle your toes and flex your ankles. Then open and close your hands; stretch out your arms. Sit up straight and take a few deep breaths. Open your eyes and engage all your senses. Let yourself focus on the sounds around you. Feel your skin tingle. Feel the energy in your body. Let your surroundings come into focus. Good job.

Now stay in *this moment* and enjoy it.

Comeback Visualization Exercise

PART 1

Lie down in bed or, if you prefer, sit comfortably with your back straight. In your mind's eye, see yourself *in the moment*—sitting on a comfortable armchair inside a dimly lit private movie theater. In front of you is a large sky blue screen that will play a video of one of your sports performances.

Imagine that you are going to review a recent competition or performance that did not go as well as it could have. Perhaps you ran slower than expected, missed an important shot, made a crucial mistake, or suffered a devastating loss. Remind yourself that this particular performance was an isolated event that does not reflect your full ability or potential. It didn't last long and will not affect other parts of your life.

Maybe the bad outing had nothing to do with your performance. That's just the way the ball bounces sometimes, and it's best to plow ahead knowing things will even out. There may have been nothing wrong with your thought process or execution. Sometimes the ball just doesn't go in, and sometimes it feels like you can't miss. If you are a shooter, your team needs you to shoot, and you need to keep taking good shots either way. Once you start hesitating and feeling like you are in a slump, that's when it actually makes it true that you're in a slump. If that sounds like your situation, this visualization exercise will help.

There may be extenuating circumstances that contributed to your performance: Perhaps your opponents were tough, it was a challenging course, or you haven't been getting enough sleep. Maybe you were just off for reasons you can't explain. This happens to everyone. So sweep all negative feelings aside and replace them with positive thoughts. Putting this setback into context while continuing to prepare yourself for your next opportunity will help you bounce back, because you know you can change the outcome next time. So picture yourself making positive changes that can affect the outcome of your next sporting event.

Think about the specifics of what happened.

- What kind of competition was this?
- Where was the competition?

- What do you remember seeing?

- Who was in the stands?

- Who was your opponent?

- What went wrong with your game plan or execution?

- If this was a team competition, who else (coaches, teammates, trainers) may have contributed to your suboptimal performance?

Next, begin to play the video on the screen and watch your performance. See yourself preparing to play as it happened on that day. What were you thinking? How were you feeling?

Now, turn your attention to the actual execution of the techniques or skills associated with your sport. Watch yourself perform. Remember your thought process and the focus that you had while competing. Recall what went wrong, but also give yourself credit for what went well.

Then notice the video rewinding to the start of your performance. Now is your chance to make the proper adjustments to help you get back on the right track. See and feel yourself performing at your peak. Just trust yourself, love your game, and enjoy your feelings. Good job!

Next, look around and see your teammates (if you play a team sport) encouraging you, and know that you support them, too. For individual-sport athletes, look around and see friends and fans supporting you. Take in your surroundings and feel the energy. Continue to feel centered and in the zone. Play out some additional successful moments in the revised game.

In a couple of moments, the video will end. Tie up loose ends. Okay, good job. We are now at the end of the first run-through of the video. Continue to imagine yourself in your private movie theater, sitting in the comfortable armchair.

PART 2

Now, in the second part of this mental exercise, instead of watching yourself on-screen, place yourself in the video and see yourself as if you are in the scenes. The only difference from Part 1 is that you are now "inside" the video.

Take your mind there now. Step into the video and begin your precompetition routine. That's right. Notice your surroundings, whether they are sights, sounds, or people. As you're visualizing your surroundings, feel that you are looking through your own eyes, listening through your own ears, and feeling the movement in your own body. You can even feel the fabric of your clothes against your skin.

As in Part 1, your competition begins. Feel what you felt while competing. Did something go wrong? How confident were you? Did you doubt your ability to compete at the appropriate level?

As earlier, rewind the video to the beginning of the competition yet notice that you are now ready to adapt and respond to any challenges. See yourself and know that you are easily able to correct any mistakes and make the adjustments necessary to get back on the right track.

In this moment, you are in complete control of your body, your state of mind, and your overall performance.

Visualize yourself going through a few more challenges or mistakes that you made. Now correct them. Perhaps you lost your composure and began to think negatively; now stay positive and patient. Perhaps your opponent made a move and you were unable to respond; now it's your turn to counter. Setbacks are your opportunity to bounce back, to make a comeback. Accept this truth: The better the competition, the more you are challenged and the more enjoyable the experience.

After moving through your challenges, return to a typical competitive scenario, moving fluidly without hesitation. Take a moment to notice everything around you.

- Your teammates are engaged in their roles, or perhaps cheering you on.
- You feel connected to them and are supporting them as well.
- You can feed off or tune out the fans as needed.
- You feel that your body is strong, full of energy, and you are mentally in the zone.

Run through a few more competitive scenarios as the video nears its conclusion. Feel the motion and pace of the competition. Let your body and intuition take over. Good job. You are now at the end of the video.

Now prepare to step back into the viewing room and sit in your comfortable armchair. Take this opportunity to reflect on what you visualized, on what was different about your game or performance.

- What went better this time?
- What were your new highlights?
- What adjustments did you make to correct your mistakes?
- How did you feel when you were at your best?

In the future, remember this feeling. To move forward, expect the best and know that you will be ready to go next competition. You have learned what it will take to perform at your best. You know that you are always one game away from being on top. You will get your game plan straightened out. You will make any adjustments to your technique or form. Fill your mind and body with confidence and determination. This is how you will build your successful comeback.

After quiet reflection, start to feel yourself in your bed or chair. Feel yourself come back to your current surroundings. Focus your attention on your feet; wiggle your toes and flex your ankles. Then open and close your hands; stretch out your arms. Sit up straight and take a few deep breaths. Open your eyes and engage all your senses. Let yourself focus on the sounds around you. Feel your skin tingle. Feel the energy in your body. Let your surroundings come into focus. Good job.

Now stay in *this moment* and enjoy it.

Marathon Visualization Exercise

Imagine lying down in the park or in your backyard on a quiet, sunny day. Feel the sun's heat on your forehead as any tension melts away. The sunlight pours onto your eyelids, which become heavy with warmth. Sense the energy of the sunshine expanding through your body. The sunlight rolls down your shoulders and flows through your back. Your back relaxes. Breathe in deeply. With every breath, you are filled with light and warmth. In this stillness, you are calm and comfortable. Enjoy this moment.

Now visualize arriving early at a marathon starting area. Spectators and competitors are moving about. Signs and barricades divide the spectators from the athletes. You look around to orient yourself. You are about to run 26.2 miles, stride by stride.

This event means a lot to you. Feeling totally powerful and unstoppable, you are about to race your best. You're happy and satisfied with the training you've put in. All your effort has made the here and now—*now*.

Your calm prerace mind-set transforms into the focused mind-set of an elite runner. Walk to the starting area and enjoy the bustling of the crowd and the energy surrounding the other runners. Absorb the energy and excitement of the impending competition. Smile at your friends and family. See the flags in front of the starting area and see the starting line. It's time to run. You're primed and destined to race your best.

Concentrate on this race—stay in the moment. Enter your starting gate; narrow your focus and expand your breathing. React to the starting gun without thinking and let motion flow into your body—a steady start followed by relaxed and well-paced strides. Your prerace plan is now an in-race plan. You shed all negativity and discomfort with one stride: the first stride. Maintain an easy pace, knowing that you started strong and will finish stronger.

"Take one mile at a time" is a cliché for a good reason: It's true. Forget past times and personal bests and only remember how good it feels *now* to be running strong. Each mile is the first mile of a new marathon (26 in a row, and then just a bit more). Be committed to the simplicity of "see, trust, run"—all race long. Run free and smooth and accept that you can only race *your* race. Commit to each mile, run within yourself, let your steady strides carry you along, and trust in your training, talent, and mind.

No other runners can pressure you. Just forget them and enjoy the simplicity of running smoothly. Allow your body to do what you've trained it to do. Know that you're strong physically, mentally, and emotionally. You are outrunning the two imposters: doubt and discomfort. You know what you did to prepare. Could you have done more? Yes, if you gave up sleep and sanity. You did what you could do and now accept that rest times are as important as relentless practice. A rested mind is ready to let you be you. Accept that you have what it takes *right now*.

Stay on course and expect something good to happen. If a good and/or bad running patch emerges, accept the good one or both equally. You are prepared to handle anything. Focus on how great your strides feel and then run fearlessly like you did as a kid—*be that kid.* You have trained for this moment, so now run *in the moment.* Simple? Should be. Let simplicity stay simple. Do not make hard what need not be hard. Don't do it.

Each mile is your first mile, and with confidence and a *quiet mind,* you're going to go farther. You already know that a consistent mental approach—stride by stride, all day, every mile—lets your training guide you to success. The keys to performing your best are simple unless you make them hard, and you won't. Say to yourself, "One mile at a time, run like a champion, accept what happens" and then repeat, repeat, repeat.

As you run, at times the surrounding noise and haste may distract you. When you feel any distraction, tone down the crowd, stay in your own world, and follow your race plan. Instinct is what drives you now, so let it flow. While other runners tighten up, pace poorly at the beginning, or hit the wall before the end—you're having fun. Stay in your own inner stillness, which lets you find your easy speed, stride by stride, and reach the finish in your own time, for your own victory.

You may encounter unexpected race conditions, and other runners may falter, complain, and get uptight. Silence them in your mind and stay in your zone. Having fun is the prelude to having your best performance. Your mind is in control, not the clock or conditions. A still and quiet mind is your racer's edge.

Love the challenge of accepting the simplicity of your running, your path, and your purpose. Nothing else matters. As you run farther, you get calmer. As each well-executed mile passes, let it go and enjoy the next stride.

As you pass the 20-mile mark, let the zone come to you as you keep it simple by letting your training, intuition, and athleticism take over. You're running, which is a form of playing. So be a runner for the sheer joy of running.

Now your final stretch approaches. Tell yourself that your final racing goal is the same as your first racing goal: confidence and a quiet mind. You're already a winner. If you stay focused within every mile, then you will inevitably perform your best. See it, feel it, and trust it as you run smoothly across the finish line.

As a sense of accomplishment floods over you, smile and give high fives to other runners. Listen to family and friends cheering. All of this is enjoyable, so pause to absorb how relaxed you were from the start to the finish, how much fun you had, and how much you trusted yourself.

Expect more races like this one, because you're going to keep running simple. Why? Because having fun is seeing and running and letting excellence happen. Anything you can envision is possible and doable. If you can see the best times, then you'll get the best times. See success, trust yourself, and prevail.

Now slowly take in a couple of deep breaths. Wiggle your toes and shake your hands. As you breathe in, prepare to return to the moment. Open your eyes and refocus. Take a deep breath and move on to the next race.

Swimming Visualization Exercise

Imagine lying down in the park or in your backyard on a quiet, sunny day. Feel the sun's heat on your forehead as any tension melts away. The sunlight pours onto your eyelids, which become heavy with warmth. Sense the energy of the sunshine expanding through your body. The sunlight rolls down your shoulders and flows through your back. Your back relaxes. Breathe in deeply. With every breath, you are filled with light and warmth. In this stillness, you are calm and comfortable. Enjoy this moment.

Now visualize arriving at the pool for a major competition—this meet means a lot because you're a competitor and now it's time to swim your best. Feeling totally powerful and unstoppable, just be happy that you are a fast swimmer destined to be a champion. Feel the satisfaction after thousands of hours of practice that makes the here and now—*now.*

In the locker room, as you change into your swimsuit also change into being an elite swimmer. Walk to the pool's deck and enjoy the crowd and the other swimmers. Absorb the energy and excitement of the impeding competition. Smile at your friends and family. See the flags in front of the starting blocks and the black line on the bottom of the pool—it's time to race.

Concentrate on this race—stay in the moment. On the starting block, focus and breathe. When the horn sounds, react without thinking—a blazing start followed by effortless strokes. Your pre-race plan is now an in-race plan. All negativity and discomfort are sinking in your wake. Maintain an easy speed, explode off the turns, and power to the wall on the last lap, knowing that you started strong and will finish stronger.

"Take one race at a time" is the oldest cliché for a reason: It's the truest. Forget past times and personal bests and only remember how good it feels *now*—win or lose—to be a superior swimmer. Each race is the first race of a new meet. Be committed to the simplicity of "see, trust, do"—all meet long. Swim free and fast and accept that you can only race *your* race. Commit to each race, swim within yourself, let your strokes carry you, and trust in your training, talent, and mind.

Your opponents cannot pressure you, as only you can apply and then accept or reject that pressure. Forget them and enjoy the simplicity of swimming fast. Allow your body to do what you've trained it to do. Know that you're strong physically, mentally, and emotionally. Outswim the sharks of doubt and fear. You know what you did to prepare. Could you have done more? Yes, if you gave up sleep and sanity. You did what you could do and now accept that rest times are as important as relentless practice. A rested mind is ready to let you be you. Accept that you have what it takes *right now.*

Between races, follow your routine: Towel off, breathe slowly, sip water, act confidently, and stay in your zone. Follow your plan and expect something good to happen. If you get a good and/or bad break, accept either or both. Neither matters as you know you're well prepared and destined to post your best times. Focus on how great your strokes feel and then race fearlessly like you did as a kid—*be that kid.* You have trained for this moment, so now swim this race. Simple? Yes. Let simplicity stay simple. It's only hard if you make it hard.

Each race is your first race, and with confidence and a *quiet mind,* you're ready to go faster. You already know that a consistent mental approach—race by race, all day, every meet—lets your training guide you to success. The keys to winning are simple, unless you make them hard, and you won't. Say to yourself, "One race at a time, swim like a champion, accept the results" and then repeat, repeat, repeat.

Amid the noise and haste, you tone down the hyper crowd, stay in your own world, and follow your routine. Keep trusting your instincts and just flow. Let the other swimmers tighten up, pace poorly at the beginning, or sink at the end—you're having fun having fun. Stay in your own inner stillness, which lets you find your top speed race by race and find the wall in your own time.

There will be unexpected race conditions, so let your opponents complain and get uptight. Ignore them and stay in your zone. Having fun is the prelude to having your best performance. Your mind is in control, not the timers' watches. A still and quiet mind is your racer's edge.

Love the challenge of accepting the simplicity of you, your lane, and your purpose. Nothing else matters. As you swim faster, you get calmer. With each well-executed lap, just let go and enjoy the next stroke. Let the zone come to you, and it will if you simplify by letting your training, intuition, and athleticism take over. You're swimming, which is a form of playing. So be a swimmer for the sheer joy of swimming.

Now, your final event is next. Everyone's watching and anticipating something special. Tell yourself that your final racing goal is the same as your first racing goal: confidence and a quiet mind. You're already a winner. If you stay focused within every lap, then you will inevitably win your share of races and meets. See it, feel it, and trust it as you torpedo through the water and touch the wall.

As accolades pour over you, just smile and give high fives to other swimmers. Enjoy being on the podium to receive the first-place medal. Listen to family and friends cheering. All of this is enjoyable, but pause to absorb how relaxed you were from starting block to final touch, how much fun you had, and how much you trusted yourself.

Expect more meets like this one, because you're going to keep swimming simple. Why? Because having fun is seeing and doing; then winning happens. Anything you can envision is possible and doable. If you can see the best times, then you'll get the best times. See victory, trust yourself, and prevail.

Now slowly take in a couple of deep breaths. Wiggle your toes and shake your hands. As you breathe in, prepare to return to the moment. Open your eyes and refocus. Take a deep breath and move on to the next race.

Academics Visualization Exercise

Imagine lying down in the park or in your backyard on a quiet, sunny day. Feel the sun's heat on your forehead as any tension melts away. The sunlight pours onto your eyelids, which become heavy with warmth. Sense the energy of the sunshine expanding through your body. The sunlight rolls down your shoulders and flows through your back. Your back relaxes. Breathe in deeply. With every breath, you are filled with light and warmth. In this stillness, you are calm and comfortable. Enjoy this moment.

Now visualize arriving at your campus and being surrounded by other students making their way to class. You feel proud of your school performance and very confident and sure of yourself because you know this is where *you want to be*. You know you can learn and perform well. You are not afraid of being unique by going the extra mile in your studies. So enjoy this feeling of satisfaction. You know that all of your efforts are turning you into a scholar people admire.

You always show up at your classes, whether you feel like it or not. *You are still on time and on mind.* As part of your preparation, you have put all personal concerns into your mental locker so that when you step into the classroom you are fully present *in the moment* and ready to learn and participate. Take slow, deep breaths to clear your mind. Picture yourself sitting near the front of the class, paying attention, asking questions, and taking good notes.

On all assignments, your intelligence and hard work lead to good grades. In contrast to many others, you understand and accept that there are no shortcuts or magic tricks in academics. You refuse to cut corners when it comes to your education. You listen to your classmates say they're not good at this or that task, but you believe that you can excel at any subject if you just put your mind to it. Hard assignments aren't too hard for you because:

- You ask questions during classes.

- You team up with other serious students with a positive approach by forming study groups so everyone can help each other master the material.

- You visit your teachers during office hours when you need additional support.

- You disassociate from others who drag you down or distract you from your studies.

Now imagine you are taking an exam or applying to a highly selective school. You feel happy, filled with joy, because you enjoy the challenge. You see yourself writing an excellent essay or confidently answering exam questions. As you use the tools that work best for you, be they pen and paper or a computer, you are ready to communicate and respond to the challenge. Your mind is *quiet* and your body is *relaxed*. You read the questions or prompts twice and envision what needs to be done and then you do it. You have total confidence that your thinking and visualization skills are the best.

Missing a few points, getting a question wrong, or writing a confusing draft does not bother you in the least because you know that going through this process will help you learn and do better next time. You accept feedback and rethink easily and quickly. You savor how good it feels to be a solid student in the game of learning and scholarship.

This you know with certainty: You are mentally and emotionally strong—a rock. Nothing bothers you or upsets you for long—*if at all.* Making mistakes or misunderstanding a concept means nothing in the long term. You do not see having to rethink or rewrite an assignment as failure. You *play* each opportunity for what it is—a new chance to win. Therefore, you never waver from your commitment to be a champion in the classroom.

You make school a sport and compete in the classroom by viewing assignments and exams as challenges to meet rather than threats to avoid. You enjoy doing what you need to do *to win*, rather than what to do *not to lose*. You quickly bounce back from all setbacks. Competition, along with cooperation, makes everyone better. You enjoy playing the game called school.

Between classes, you talk with your instructor or learning partners. You feel comfortable and know you belong. *This is where you want to be.* At all times, you expect something good to happen, and you know it will. Then it does.

- You get the good grade you knew was coming because you have worked hard and intelligently.

- You know you are destined to be successful in this course, lab, or semester.

- You look for any opportunity to improve and for any unique piece of information or understanding to use to your advantage.

- You enjoy how great you feel and savor the joy of understanding what you intend to do and want to know.

Learning is now your passion.

You consider new ideas with a joyful mind and a playful mood. You are doing what you love, but remind yourself that the real goal is maintaining a positive attitude every step of the way. You see each problem and accept it, mindful of the details. You trust in your abilities and talent.

You now know you can do many things and do them well.

Infinite patience, although often tested, guides you because you have a *quiet* mind. You start assignments by knowing how you will approach with an open and focused mind every detail and idea, and this prior knowledge gives you ample self-confidence. You know that if you approach each learning process in the same way and trust yourself, then you will succeed. This is the key to winning the game of learning. Play one shot at a time just like a golfer, accept feedback and results, and learn.

You have a game plan.

• Study each day rather than cramming before an exam.

• Train your mind to be in work mode at the same time each day. This approach helps you learn and retain information.

• Keep your schoolwork and room organized.

• Feel good because you stick to this rule: *Do not fall behind.*

• If there are other students complaining about assignments and procrastinating, briefly notice this and then actively ignore it. You are having *fun with a purpose.*

• Love the opportunity and enjoy the challenge.

• Learn what you want to know and enjoy the journey.

• Smile and feel satisfied as you earn good grades on all exams and papers. See yourself telling this good news to family and friends.

• Enjoy this feeling and be proud of how hard you worked throughout this process, how much fun you had, and how much you trusted yourself.

Know this: You are going to enjoy more good results and good days because you will always make learning *fun*. Why? Because now you know that when you are having fun and doing your absolute best, good grades follow. That's the best strategy for success at school. Anything your mind can conceive is possible . . . after you simply let yourself do it.

Now very slowly, take a couple of deep breaths and come back *into the moment* and get started on your successful future.

Workplace Visualization Exercise

Imagine lying down in the park or in your backyard on a quiet, sunny day. Feel the sun's heat on your forehead as any tension melts away. The sunlight pours onto your eyelids, which become heavy with warmth. Sense the energy of the sunshine expanding through your body. The sunlight rolls down your shoulders and flows through your back. Your back relaxes. Breathe in deeply. With every breath, you are filled with light and warmth. In this stillness, you are calm and comfortable. Enjoy this moment.

Now visualize being at your workplace and being surrounded by your colleagues. You feel very proud of your performance and very confident and sure of yourself because you know this is where *you want to be*. You know you can learn and perform well. You are not afraid of being unique by going the extra mile in your work responsibilities. Enjoy this feeling of satisfaction. You know that all of your efforts are turning you into a professional people admire.

You always prepare for meetings. *You are on time and on mind.* When you step into the office or boardroom, you put all personal concerns into your mental desk drawer so that you are fully present *in the moment* and ready to contribute. Take slow, deep breaths to clear your mind. Picture yourself in meetings paying attention, asking questions, and taking good notes.

You earn good daily, periodic, and annual evaluations through your intelligently applied hard work. You understand that there are no shortcuts or magic tricks in the workplace. You refuse to cut corners when it comes to your career. You listen to your colleagues say they're not good at this or that task, but you believe that you will excel in any area if you just put your mind to it. Hard work isn't too hard for you because:

- You ask questions during meetings.

- You team up with other serious colleagues with a positive approach by forming work groups so everyone can help each other master their unique challenges.

- You call on your colleagues whenever you need additional support.

- You disassociate from others who are dragging you down or distracting you from your work.

Now imagine you are completing a job that is widely perceived as difficult. Yet you feel happy, filled with joy, because you enjoy the challenge. You clearly see yourself writing an excellent report. As you use the tools that work best for you, be they pen and paper or a computer, you are ready to communicate and respond to the challenge. Your mind is *quiet* and your body is *relaxed*. You read the directions twice, the prompt for the assignment, and envision what needs to be done. Then you do it. You have total confidence that your thinking and visualization skills are the best.

Missing a few points or writing a confusing draft doesn't bother you in the least because you know that going through this process will help you learn and do better next time. You accept revisions and rethink easily and quickly. You savor how good it feels to be a solid professional in the game of learning and working.

This you know with certainty: You are strong mentally and emotionally—a rock. Nothing bothers you or upsets you for long—*if at all*. Making mistakes or misunderstanding a concept means nothing in the long term. You do not fear failure in seeing an idea differently or having to rethink or rewrite an assignment. You play each opportunity for what it is—a new chance to win. Therefore, you never waver from your commitment to be a champion in the boardroom.

You make work a sport and compete in the boardroom by viewing your job as a wealth of challenges to meet rather than threats to avoid. You enjoy doing what you need to do *to win*, rather than what to do *not to lose*. You quickly bounce back from all setbacks. Competition, along with cooperation, makes everyone better. You enjoy playing the game called work.

Between meetings, you talk with your colleagues, feeling comfortable and knowing you belong. *This is where you want to be.* At all times, you expect something good to happen and you know it will. Then it does.

• You get the good review you knew was coming because you worked hard and intelligently.

• You know you are destined to successfully complete this important task.

• You look for any opportunity to improve and for any unique piece of information or understanding to use to your advantage.

• You *enjoy* how great you feel and the joy that comes with understanding.

Excellence is now your passion.

You consider new ideas with a joyful mind and a playful mood. You are doing what you love, but remind yourself that the real goal is maintaining a positive attitude every step of the way. You see each problem and accept it, mindful of the details. You trust in your abilities and talent.

You now know you can do many things and do them well.

Infinite patience, although often tested, guides you because you have a *quiet* mind. You start work tasks by knowing how you will approach with an open and focused mind every detail and idea, and this prior knowledge gives you ample self-confidence. You know that if you approach each learning process the same way, by trusting yourself, then you will succeed. This is the key to winning the game of work. Play one shot at a time just like a golfer, accept feedback and results, and learn what you need to be successful.

You have a game plan.

• Get work done each day rather than cramming before a deadline.

• Train your mind to be in work mode at the same time each day. This approach helps you learn and retain information.

• Keep your paperwork and office organized.

• Feel good because you stick to this rule: *Do not fall behind.*

• If there are others around complaining about work and pro-crastinating, briefly notice this and then actively ignore it. You are having *fun with a purpose.*

• Love the opportunity and enjoy the challenge.

• Learn what you want to know and enjoy the journey.

• Smile and feel satisfied as you earn good reviews on all projects and assignments. See yourself telling this good news to family and friends.

• Enjoy this feeling and be proud of how hard you worked throughout this process, how much fun you had, and how much you trusted yourself.

Know this: You will *enjoy* more good results and good days because you will always make working *fun.* Why? Because now you know that when you are having fun and doing your absolute best, good results follow. That's the best strategy for success at work. Anything your mind can conceive is possible . . . after you simply let yourself do it.

Now very slowly, take a couple of deep breaths and come back *into the moment* and get started on your successful future.

Fitness Visualization Exercise

Imagine lying down in the park or in your backyard on a quiet, sunny day. Feel the sun's heat on your forehead as any tension melts away. The sunlight pours onto your eyelids, which become heavy with warmth. Sense the energy of the sunshine expanding through your body. The sunlight rolls down your shoulders and flows through your back. Your back relaxes. Breathe in deeply. With every breath, you are filled with light and warmth. In this stillness, you are calm and comfortable. Enjoy this moment.

Now visualize arriving at your gym and being surrounded by others already working out. You feel proud of your commitment to fitness and confident because you know this is where *you want to be*. You know you can learn and perform well. You are not afraid of being unique by going the extra mile in your fitness routine. So enjoy this feeling of satisfaction. You know that all of your efforts are turning you into an athlete people admire.

You always show up at your gym or fitness class, whether you feel like it or not. *You are on time and on mind.* You have put all personal concerns into your mental locker. When you step onto the floor, you are fully present *in the moment* and ready to work out. Take slow, deep breaths to clear your mind. Picture yourself beginning your warmup routine, deciding what you want to accomplish during your workout, and being ready for this opportunity.

You perform well in all exercises, lifts, and movements because you put in high-quality effort. You understand and accept that there are no shortcuts or magic tricks in the gym. You refuse to cut corners when it comes to your workout. You believe that you can excel at any exercise if you just *put your mind to it*. Hard workouts aren't too hard for you because:

- You ask questions during fitness classes.

- You team up with other serious athletes with a positive approach in the weight room so everyone can help each other master their unique challenges.

- You visit your fitness trainer whenever you need additional support.

• You disassociate from others who are dragging you down or distracting you from your workout.

Now imagine you are executing a tough exercise routine that pushes you to your limits. Even as you reach the edge of your limits, you feel happy, filled with joy, because you enjoy the challenge and the growth at these borders of effort. You see yourself flawlessly executing lifts or moving through your routine. You use the proper techniques. You engage your body and breath to respond to each challenge. Your mind is *quiet,* your breath is *deep,* and your body is *powerful.* You prepare for the next set or rep and envision what needs to be done. Then you do it. You have total confidence that your mental focus and physical skills are at their best.

Missing a target time or struggling with a lift does not bother you in the least because you know that going through this process will help you improve. You accept feedback from your fitness trainer and modify your routine accordingly. You savor how good it feels to exercise regularly.

This you know with certainty: You are strong mentally and emotionally—a rock. Nothing bothers you or upsets you for long—*if at all.* Making mistakes or misunderstanding a concept means nothing in the long term. You do not fear failure. You are patient with your progress and understand that fine-tuning your technique or form takes time. You engage with each opportunity for what it is—a new chance to build your body. You never waver from your commitment to be a champion in fitness.

You make fitness a sport and compete with yourself in the gym, pool, or class by viewing workouts as challenges to meet rather than as threats to avoid. You enjoy learning what to do to *get stronger,* rather than fearing that you are never going to *get better.* You quickly bounce back from all setbacks. You enjoy playing the game called fitness.

Between sets or exercises, you talk with your fitness trainer or exercise partners. You feel comfortable knowing that you are making gains. *This is where you want to be.* At all times, you expect something good to happen and you know it will. Then it does.

• Your fitness level improves because you have worked hard and intelligently.

• You know you are destined to be successful in this fitness class, workout, or challenge.

• You look for any opportunity to improve and for any unique piece of information or understanding to use to your advantage.

• You enjoy how great you feel and savor the joy of accomplishing what you intend to do.

Fitness is now your passion.

You consider new ideas with a joyful mind and a playful mood. You are doing what you love, but remind yourself that the real goal is maintaining a positive attitude every step of the way. You see each challenge and accept it, mindful of the details. You trust in your abilities and talent.

You now know you can do many things and do them well.

Infinite patience, although often tested, guides you because you have a *quiet* mind. You start your workout by knowing how you will approach with an open and focused mind every detail and technique, and this prior knowledge gives you ample self-confidence. You know that if you approach each fitness challenge the same way, by trusting yourself, then you will succeed. This is the key to winning the game of fitness. Track, accept, and learn from feedback. Monitoring your journey gives you insight and provides motivation over the long term.

You have a game plan.

• Exercise regularly rather than bingeing.

• Train your mind and body to be ready to work out at the same time each day. This approach helps you stay motivated and maximizes results.

• Keep your workout gear organized and readily available.

• Feel good because you stick to this rule: *Do not fall behind.*

• If there are others around complaining about the workout, briefly notice this and then actively ignore it. You are having *fun with a purpose.*

• Love the opportunity and enjoy the challenge.

• Learn what you want to know about fitness and move forward in the journey.

• Smile and feel satisfied as you reach your fitness goals. See yourself telling this good news to family and friends.

• Enjoy this feeling and be proud of how hard you worked throughout this process, how much fun you had, and how much you trusted yourself.

Know this: You are going to enjoy more good results and good days because you will always make exercising *fun*. Why? Because now you know that when you are having fun and doing your absolute best, fitness follows. That's the best strategy for exercise success. Anything your mind can conceive is possible . . . after you simply let yourself do it. You relish regular exercise and always complete it knowing you went all in.

Take a last look around you. Be mindful of how your body feels now. Very slowly, take a couple of deep breaths, open your eyes, and come back *into the moment*. You've completed an excellent session. Now get started on your future fitness.

Injury-Recovery Visualization Exercise

Imagine lying down in the park or in your backyard on a quiet, sunny day. Feel the sun's heat on your forehead as any tension melts away. The sunlight pours onto your eyelids, which become heavy with warmth. Sense the energy of the sunshine expanding through your body. The sunlight rolls down your shoulders and flows through your back. Your back relaxes. Breathe in deeply. With every breath, you are filled with light and warmth. In this stillness, you are calm and comfortable. Enjoy this moment.

Now visualize arriving at your sports-medicine or sports-rehab clinic and take note of the equipment and staff there to help you. This is where *you need to be to get your game back*. You feel proud of your commitment to a full recovery and are confident that you will put in your best effort. You know you will learn new techniques and routines that will make you stronger. You are not afraid of being unique by sticking to your rehabilitation regimen. So enjoy this feeling of satisfaction. You know that all of your efforts are helping you make a successful return to competition as quickly and safely as possible.

You always show up at your clinic or do your rehab exercises at home, whether you feel like it or not. *You are on time and on mind.* You have put all personal concerns into your mental locker. When you begin a session, you are fully present *in the moment* and ready to rehab. Take slow, deep breaths to clear your mind. Picture yourself beginning your warmup routine, reviewing your rehab exercises, and being ready for this opportunity.

You perform well in all exercises, lifts, or movements because you put in high-quality effort. You understand and accept that there are no shortcuts or magic tricks in rehab. You refuse to cut corners when it comes to your recovery. You believe that you can excel at any exercise if you just *put your mind to it.* Hard rehab exercises aren't too hard for you because:

- You ask questions when meeting with your sports-medicine specialists to understand your injury and rehabilitation or strengthening-exercise program.

- You team up with other serious athletes with a positive approach in the training room so everyone can help each other master their unique challenges.

- You visit your sports-medicine specialists whenever you need additional support.

- You disassociate from others who are dragging you down or distracting you from your rehab.

Now imagine you are executing a tough exercise routine that pushes you to your limits. Even as you reach the edge of your limits, you feel happy, filled with joy, because you enjoy the challenge and growth at these borders of effort. You see yourself flawlessly executing lifts or moving through your routine. You use the proper techniques. You engage your body and breath to respond to each challenge. Your mind is *quiet,* your breath is *deep,* and your body is *powerful.* You prepare for the next set or rep and envision what needs to be done. Then you do it. You have total confidence that your mental focus and physical skills are at their best.

Missing a target time or struggling with a lift does not bother you in the least because you know that this informs you about your current limits. They are markers for this journey. You accept feedback from your athletic trainer and modify your routine accordingly. You savor how good it feels to identify weak areas, find movements to gain strength, and get stronger with each rehab session.

You know this with certainty: You are strong mentally and emotionally—a rock. Nothing bothers you or upsets you for long—*if at all*. Making mistakes or misunderstanding a concept means nothing in the long term. You do not fear failure. You are patient with your progress and understand that changing muscle patterns and building new movement take time. You engage with each opportunity for what it is—a new chance to give attention to your body. You never waver from your commitment to be a champion in recovery.

You make rehab a sport and compete with yourself while doing stretching routines, body-weight exercises, or resistance-band sets by viewing rehab exercises as challenges to meet rather than as threats to avoid. You enjoy learning what to do *to get stronger,* rather than fearing that you are never going to *get better.* You quickly bounce back from all setbacks. You enjoy playing the game called rehab.

Between exercises, you talk with your athletic trainer or rehab partners. You feel comfortable and know that you are making gains. You are focusing on your progress, and seeing milestones keeps you on track on this journey. *This is where you need to be to get your game back.* At all times, you expect something good to happen and you know it will. Then it does.

- Your strength and range of motion improve because you have worked hard and intelligently.

- You know you are destined to be successful in this rehabilitation.

- You look for any opportunity to improve and for any unique piece of information or understanding to use to your advantage.

- You enjoy how great you feel and savor the joy of accomplishing what you intend to do.

Rehab is now your passion.

You consider new ideas with a joyful mind and a playful mood. You are doing what you have to do, but remind yourself that the real goal is maintaining a positive attitude every step of the way. You see each challenge and accept it, mindful of the details. You trust in your abilities and talent.

You now know you can do many things and do them well.

Infinite patience, although often tested, guides you because you have a *quiet* mind. You start your rehab session by knowing how you will approach with an open and focused mind every detail and technique, and this prior knowledge gives you ample self-confidence. You know that if you approach each phase of rehabilitation the same way, by trusting yourself, then you will succeed. This is the key to winning the game of rehabilitation. Track, accept, and learn from feedback. Monitoring your journey gives you insight and provides motivation over the long term.

You have a game plan.

- Rehab regularly rather than skipping sessions or doing too much too soon.

• Train your mind and body to be ready to do your rehab at the same time each day. This approach helps you stay motivated and maximizes results.

• Keep your rehabilitation equipment organized and readily available.

• Feel good because you stick to this rule: *Do not fall behind.*

• If there are others around complaining about their rehabilitation, briefly notice this and then actively ignore it. You are having *fun with a purpose.*

• Love the opportunity and enjoy the challenge.

• Learn what you want to know about your injury and move forward in the journey.

• Smile and feel satisfied as you regain increased movement, range of motion, and strength. See yourself telling this good news to family and friends.

• Enjoy this feeling and be proud of how hard you worked throughout this process, how much fun you had, and how much you trusted yourself.

Know this: You are going to enjoy more good results and good days because you make rehab fun. Why? Because now you know that when you are having fun and doing your absolute best, recovery follows. That's the best strategy for rehabilitation success. Anything your mind can conceive is possible . . . after you simply let yourself do it. You relish regular rehab exercise and always complete it knowing you went all in.

Take a last look around you. Be mindful of how your body feels now. Very slowly, take a couple of deep breaths, open your eyes, and come back *into the moment.* You have completed an excellent session and made further progress in your recovery.

THE FINAL TAKEAWAY

Visualization is an indispensable tool, just like shooting drills and practice on a basketball court. Scores of experimental studies and anecdotal evidence have backed the benefits of using visualization for performance enhancement. This tool, if consistently practiced, builds a bridge between the mental and the physical. You'll be able to see the victory and then achieve it.

CHAPTER EIGHT

THE 300 CLUB

Spartans! Prepare for glory!

—GERARD BUTLER AS KING LEONIDAS IN *300*

The movie *300*, directed by Zack Snyder, was released in 2006. It is an adaptation of the 1998 Frank Miller and Lynn Varley comic series that recounts the historical battle of Thermopylae between Greece and Persia (modern-day Iran) in 480 BC.

The story goes as follows: Regional superpower Persia seeks to expand its empire. The mighty Persian army is led by the god-king Xerxes (Rodrigo Santoro). The only obstacle in Xerxes's path is Leonidas (Gerard Butler), the king of the Greek city-state of Sparta, and his band of vastly outnumbered warriors. Though imminent death awaits these Spartans, their courage and sacrifice inspires all of the Greek city-states to unite against their common enemy.

In a now-famous scene, a Persian messenger warns the Spartans that unless they surrender, "a thousand nations of the Persian empire [will] descend upon you. Our arrows will blot out the sun!" A young, brave Spartan soldier named Stelios (Michael Fassbender) smiles at the messenger and responds, "Then we will fight in the shade." To maintain their dignity and freedom, the Spartans refuse to back down despite the horrendous odds.

In your own game, be equally confident in your abilities to beat the odds and achieve your goals. Remember that the harder the adversity or the bigger the setbacks, the more opportunities to learn and the more glory to be gained upon a successful comeback. In this chapter, we will look inside the minds of three champions to examine how they reached the pinnacle of their professions, made remarkable comebacks, and refused to back down even when victory seemed out of reach.

FROM FIZZO TO FINAL FOURS

We'll play anybody, anyplace, anytime. It doesn't matter, morning, noon, or night, and it doesn't matter who it is.

—TOM IZZO

Tom Izzo, head coach of the Michigan State men's basketball team, has certainly embraced the "Spartan Way." He was born and raised in Iron Mountain, a small city in the Upper Peninsula of Michigan. In this blue-collar city, the Izzo family was no exception. At the age of 12, Tom learned about hard work at Izzo's Shoe Hospital, a business owned by his father and uncle.

A self-described jack-of-all-trades, Tom learned to fix shoes and do a host of other handyman services. Tom's grandfather was still working in the shop at the age of 90. Seventeen of his grandchildren, and eventually 13 of his great-grandchildren, worked there through the years. Izzo learned to value family and work at Izzo's Shoe Hospital, and those are his two priorities now.

Iron Mountain is about 100 miles from Green Bay, Wisconsin. Vince Lombardi coached the Green Bay Packers to five NFL championships (including the first two Super Bowls) during the 1960s and had a big impact on Izzo's life. Izzo read Lombardi's books and studied his coaching philosophy.

In Iron Mountain, Tom met his best friend, future NFL head coach Steve Mariucci. Both attended Iron Mountain High, where they were teammates on the football, basketball, and track teams. Izzo was recruited by football programs, but he loved basketball and decided to walk on at Northern Michigan University (NMU) in Marquette.

Mariucci also matriculated to NMU, and he and Izzo became roommates. Mariucci was a two-time All-American quarterback and guided NMU to the NCAA Division II National Championship. Izzo played guard for the Wildcats' basketball team from 1973 to 1977. In his senior season, he set a school record for minutes played and was selected as a Division II All-American.

After graduating from NMU, Izzo served as head basketball coach at Michigan's Ishpeming High School for one season. He then took an assistant coaching job at his alma mater from 1979 to 1983. Next, Izzo landed in East Lansing at Michigan State University (MSU) as a part-time assistant for coach Jud Heathcote. Heathcote coached a total of 19 years at MSU, including a national championship 1979 season that featured star player and local legend Magic Johnson.

At MSU, Izzo became a tireless worker and excellent recruiter. His efforts and loyalty paid off handsomely when Heathcote promoted him to associate head coach prior to the 1990–91 season. After Heathcote's retirement following the 1994–95 season, he recommended Izzo as his replacement. This was not a popular decision at the time, especially as Izzo had limited head-coaching experience.

Izzo's tenure as head coach at MSU got off to a slow start. Around this time, I started graduate school at MSU to study sports psychology and counseling. The local media and Spartans fans were not pleased with the team missing the NCAA tournament during Izzo's first 2 years. In fact, I remember attending games at the Breslin Center and noticing that some disgruntled fans in the student section held signs that read FIZZO.

Years later, Izzo shared a story about making the mistake of turning on the radio during the team's subpar 4–3 start to the 1997–98 season. Izzo and his assistant coach, Tom Crean, were out at lunch when they heard a local sports show drilling Izzo's performance and claiming that the question wasn't *if* Izzo was going to get fired, but *when*.

Izzo says that he'll remember what happened next until the day he dies. He returned to his office and had a big meeting with his staff, including the athletic trainers, strength coach, and secretaries. Rather than retreating into a shell, Izzo looked for support and built a winning program. The Spartans turned things around right away. Behind sophomore point guard sensation Mateen Cleaves, MSU went 18–5 for the remainder of the season to tie for first place in the Big Ten Conference and then reached the Sweet 16 in the NCAA tournament.

During the 1998–99 season, the Spartans went 15–1 in the conference to capture the Big Ten crown. They stayed hot during March Madness and reached the NCAA Final Four, finishing with a 33–5 overall record. Unfortunately, they fell short of their ultimate goal: the national championship. Cleaves had a great opportunity to enter the NBA draft after his junior season, but he and Izzo had an epic comeback in mind.

The Spartans would not be denied in the 1999–2000 season. They tied for first in the Big Ten and won the NCAA Championship, beating Florida 89–76. Morris Peterson led the Spartans with 21 points. Cleaves suffered a serious ankle injury in the second half of the championship game but still managed to score 18 points and add four assists. He was named the Final Four Most Outstanding Player.

Fast-forward to the start of the 2014–15 season. Under Izzo, the Spartans had won a national championship, played in 6 Final Fours, claimed 7 Big Ten championships, and earned invitations to 17 consecutive NCAA tournaments. The Spartans had finished the 2013–14 season with a loss to Connecticut—the eventual national champions—in the Elite Eight of the NCAA tournament.

Although the 2014–15 team was lacking in talent, without All-Americans or surefire future lottery or first-round picks, "Tournament Tom" had another major comeback in mind. He scheduled a grueling nonconference schedule to prepare his team for the NCAA tournament. Izzo is known for two mottos: "Players play and tough players win" and "I don't determine playing time, players do." He has a participatory leadership style and wants his players to take ownership. Here's Izzo on the importance of ownership.

> If people take ownership of something, they have a better chance to be successful. If players think they are simply doing something for you or the school, they will do it, but it is not ownership. I take the same approach with

coaches. You cannot ask a guy to work 18 hours a day if it just benefits you. I believe if they trust in themselves and have ownership, they feel better about themselves and they do a better job.

The team would need to take ownership and squeeze every ounce out of themselves to make something big happen. The 2014–15 Spartans finished the regular season tied for third in the Big Ten, were ranked 23rd by the Associated Press, and were invited to their 18th straight NCAA tournament. Although Izzo acknowledged that this was not a "vintage Michigan State team," and they were seeded No. 7 in the East Regional, he was optimistic about advancing deep into the tournament. In the first round, the Spartans beat No. 10 seed Georgia Bulldogs 70–63.

Next the Spartans faced No. 2 seed Virginia Cavaliers (ranked No. 6 overall in the country). Izzo gave his players an epic pregame speech, with a special message for his seniors, which was broadcast by CBS Sports.

> You live for these games, guys. It's why you coach. You live for these games. I think of my three seniors this morning when I got up. I think of where [Branden Dawson] and [Travis Trice], you were; [Keenan Wetzel], where you are. To think that you played on an aircraft carrier as freshmen, you played in Germany as a sophomore, you played to go to a Final Four as a junior. You've played on some of the biggest, most unique stages that the game of basketball has to offer. It's time to take one more step, guys. You deserve to take one more step, but it's going to take every bit of focus, communication, and concentration you have. Nothing more than [what] should be expected.

As you move up in this tournament, that's what matters: focus, communication, attention to detail. All the little things are going to matter. Let's go out there!

The Spartans stunned the Cavaliers 60–54 to *take one more step*. Next up for MSU was No. 3 Oklahoma in the Sweet 16, and the Spartans won that game, 62–58, to *take one more step*. In the Elite Eight, MSU played against No. 4 seed Louisville. Before the game, Izzo had another simple message for his players.

> I only have one message for you here. One message, one message only: two hours. Two hours, you do everything you can do for two hours. Two hours out of the millions of hours you guys have worked out when you think about it. Just give me two hours, and you're going to have 50, 60, 70 years of memories. Two hours. Can you sacrifice and reach down and give me two hours so you can have memories for you, your family, your kids, and your kids' kids.

The Spartans came back from an eight-point halftime deficit to defeat the Cardinals in overtime, 76–70, to extend their improbable run and reach the Final Four. Louisville had won 94 straight games when leading by at least six points at halftime. Izzo became the first coach to take three teams seeded No. 5 or lower to the Final Four.

Despite MSU's loss to Duke, the eventual national champions, Izzo said that this Final Four trip, his seventh, might have been the most special. It was certainly the most improbable. "This team gave me everything they had to give me and they played through so many things," Izzo said.

So what are *you* going to do for a lifetime of *your* memories?

HOGAN MAJORED IN COMEBACKS

*As you walk down the fairway of life, you must smell the roses,
for you only get to play one round.*

—BEN HOGAN

It was a foggy early morning 200 miles outside of El Paso, Texas, on February 2, 1949. Professional golfer Ben Hogan and his wife, Valerie, were heading back to their home in Fort Worth from Arizona, where Hogan had played in the Phoenix Open.

A Greyhound bus attempting to pass a truck on an icy bridge crossed the center line and collided head-on with Hogan's Cadillac. A split second before the crash, Hogan, who was driving, threw himself across the seat in front of Valerie to protect her from the impact.

His valiant attempt to save his wife saved both of them, as the steering wheel slammed into the driver's seat. Valerie sustained cuts and bruises and Hogan suffered a multitude of serious injuries, including a fractured pelvis, a broken collarbone, a chipped rib, a left ankle fracture, and near-fatal blood clots. It was 90 minutes after the accident before an ambulance finally arrived.

After the accident, Hogan spent 59 days recuperating in the hospital. A blood clot in his left leg required a critical operation. He was encased in a thick cast that went from his hips to his armpits. His injuries from the wreck were so severe that doctors said he might have difficulty walking. Competitive golf did not seem to be in the cards.

At the time of the accident, Hogan was 36 years old and in the prime of his career. During his recovery, he had ample time to reflect on his life. He had been tested too many times to be discouraged now and give up on professional golf. As writer C. S. Lewis said, "Hardship often prepares an ordinary person for an extraordinary destiny."

William Ben Hogan was born in Stephenville, Texas, on August 13, 1912. He was the youngest of Clara and Chester Hogan's three children. His family later moved to Fort Worth. In 1922, when Hogan was 9, his father committed suicide by self-inflicted gunshot. Ben witnessed the horrific event.

After Chester's suicide, the family was in dire financial straits. To help make ends meet, the children took jobs to supplement their mother's income as a seamstress. Hogan's 14-year-old brother, Royal, quit school and became a deliveryman, transporting office supplies by bicycle. After school, Ben sold newspapers at the local train station.

A suggestion from a friend led 11-year-old Ben to the Glen Garden Country Club, a nine-hole course 7 miles south of town. Ben became a caddy. One of his fellow caddies was Byron Nelson, later a PGA Tour rival. They battled at the annual Christmas caddy tournament in December 1927, when both were 15. Nelson sank a 30-foot putt to tie on the ninth and final hole. They played another nine holes; Nelson drained a long putt on the final green to win by a stroke.

Hogan had the golf bug and continued to work hard on his game. At age 17, he turned professional at the 1930 Texas Open in San Antonio. To help pay bills, he took a low-paying club pro job in 1932. He married Valerie Fox in 1935. In the ensuing years, Hogan went broke on several occasions.

He struggled mightily during his early years as a pro, when he fought a bad hook. He compared holding his driver to holding a rattlesnake. Yet his wife believed in him, and her support encouraged him to keep practicing hard. He eventually overcame his hook by perfecting a picture-perfect fade, "digging it out of the dirt" through relentless practice and experimentation.

Hogan was on the tour for a decade before his game fully blossomed. In 1940, he won his first pro tournament, the prestigious North and South Open at Pinehurst Resort in North Carolina. He would go on to lead the tour in lowest scoring average and total earnings for 3 consecutive years.

Hogan served in the US Army Air Force from March 1943 to June 1945. His boyhood rival Byron Nelson got a medical exemption and in 1945 went on his famous streak of 11 wins in a row and 18 wins in a year. Nelson was taking over the tour, and the media began referring to him as "Mr. Golf."

On September 30, 1945, Hogan fired a final-round 64 to win the Portland Open Invitational at the Portland Golf Club in Oregon. He set a PGA Tour record for a 72-hole event by shooting 27 under par. Nelson finished in second place 14 shots back. Fellow tour player Jimmy Demaret hurried over to congratulate Hogan. Without missing a beat, the stoic Hogan said to Demaret, "I guess that takes care of this 'Mr. Golf' business."

In 1946, Hogan won his first major, the PGA Championship. In 1948, he captured two more majors, the US Open and his second PGA Championship. In the 1940s, Hogan won an astounding 53 tournaments. Then in 1949, the accident. He survived the head-on collision, but his golf career seemed all but ended. He would be crippled the rest of his life, or so his doctors thought. They didn't know that Hogan was 16 months away from making one of the greatest comebacks in sports history.

The 1950 US Open was held June 8 through 11 at the East Course of Merion Golf Club near Philadelphia. Hogan put himself within striking range after scoring a 72 in the first round. The second round on a Saturday was a 36-hole double round. Could Hogan stand up under the punishment? His legs were still battered and tightly wrapped and he had difficulty walking. Hogan had a three-stroke lead, but on the 12th tee of his second 18, his body broke down. As he drove the ball, his legs locked and he nearly fell. He staggered to a friend in the gallery. "My God," he uttered. "I don't think I can finish." Gathering himself, Hogan endured the pain and soldiered on.

After a bogey on the 12th hole, Hogan did his best to hang on through the remaining six holes. His lead evaporated after another bogey on the 17th. On the 18th hole, he needed a par to earn his way into a playoff. Hogan split the fairway with his drive, but it was woefully short, leaving him 213 yards to the flag. On his second shot, Hogan ripped a 1-iron to within 40 feet of the hole. His follow-through on that swing, captured in a famous photograph, has become an iconic image in golf history. He proceeded to two-putt for par to get into the three-way Sunday playoff with local star George Fazio and Lloyd Mangrum, the 1946 US Open champion.

The following day, the press and public swarmed to see if Hogan could pull off the incredible. On the first nine, Hogan and Mangrum both shot 36 to share the lead. Fazio shot one over par. The gallery cheered Hogan on. At the 18th green, Hogan was one putt away from what seemed impossible. He sank the putt and won the playoff by four strokes over Mangrum and six strokes over Fazio. The 1950 US Open was mainly a victory of Hogan's unyielding will. In those 4 demanding days, Ben Hogan proved he was still the greatest.

Here are the strategies Hogan used, organized according to the Champion's Comeback Code.

• **LET GO:** To release mental bricks, Hogan maintained his perspective. "Well, that's why they make 18 holes," Hogan once said about double-bogeying the first hole at a tournament that he would go on to win. He understood that "golf is not a game of perfect," as sports psychologist Bob Rotella later described it. Hogan's emphasis was always on the next shot, because that is always the most important shot.

• **LOOK FOR SUPPORT:** Hogan's wife, Valerie, was his best friend and greatest supporter. After the accident, he was also buoyed by the tremendous outpouring of support from fans he never realized he had. After his career ended, Hogan explained, "I didn't know that many people knew me and wanted me to continue, and I think that played a great part in my determination to come back and play again. And I certainly wanted to come back and win again, not only for myself and Valerie, but for the people who wrote me and were interested. I'm so pleased and thankful to have found this out. Golf was my life and I didn't want to give it up, so I went back to work."

• **LOVE THE GAME:** Hogan practiced and played with purpose and passion. There wasn't enough daylight for him to practice and play as much as he would have liked. "Golf to me is . . . a livelihood in doing the thing that I like to do. I don't like the glamour. I just like the game."

• **LEARN:** Hogan embraced a growth mind-set throughout his career, learning as much as possible about the swing and the game of golf. While working as a caddy, he learned to play the game from Ed Stewart, the best player at Glen Garden. Throughout his career, Hogan also observed the best players and attempted to emulate them. He said that he never played a round without learning something new. "The greatest pleasure is obtained by improving," he said.

• **LABOR:** Known as golf's hardest, most diligent worker on the driving range, Hogan dedicated himself to keep pounding the rock on a daily basis by working hard and smart on his swing from sunrise to sunset. "I always outworked everybody. Work never bothered me like it bothers some people. You can outwork the best player in the world," Hogan said.

• **LEARN OPTIMISM:** After his accident, Hogan bought into his comeback story by embracing an attitude of expectation. His new mission was to get back on top of the game. During a practice round at the 1950 US Open, Hogan told his caddy, "Carefully replace the divot, son, because I plan to be here every round." Hogan is telling him to replace the divot because he expects to hit the ball to that exact spot every round. He famously said, "There is no reason why a golfer can't birdie every hole."

• **LEAN ON YOUR MENTAL GAME:** "You outwork them, you out-think them, and then you intimidate them," Hogan said. In addition to his work ethic, Hogan separated himself from the pack with his concentration, confidence, and composure. He was a master of positive self-talk, body language, and goal setting.

Visualization was one of Hogan's favorite mental skills. He shared this with *Golf* magazine in 1987. "Even as I practiced [I was] visualizing shots and making the ball move in different ways on the range. Otherwise, it's nothing but calisthenics. When the shot I visualized didn't come off, I might hit 20 more before I got it right," Hogan said.

Hogan was famous for being in a cocoon of concentration when he played. At the 1947 Masters, Claude Harmon made a hole in one while paired with Hogan on the 12th hole. Hogan proceeded to make a birdie, and then while walking to the next hole, he turned to Harmon and said, "You know, Claude, that's the first two I've ever made on that hole." Hogan was so focused that he was unware that Harmon had just aced the hole. Or maybe he was just doing the unexpected to rattle his opponent.

After his comeback victory at Merion, Hogan would go on to win his third and fourth US Opens (1951 and 1953)—only Willie Anderson, Bobby Jones, and Jack Nicklaus have won as many—and the 1953 British Open at Carnoustie, Scotland (Hogan's only British Open appearance). After returning to New York from Scotland, Hogan was greeted with a ticker tape parade. It was the first time a golfer had been so honored since Jones in 1930. Hogan had won the Masters and US Open that same year, and five of the six tournaments in which he competed. Despite the years taken away from his career due to World War II and the car accident, Hogan amassed 64 PGA Tour wins. From 1946 to 1953, Hogan won 9 out of the 16 major competitions in which he competed.

THE COMEBACK QUEEN

A champion isn't about how much they win,
it's about how they recover from their downs.
—SERENA WILLIAMS

Serena Jameka Williams was born in Saginaw, Michigan, on September 26, 1981. She is the younger of Oracene and Richard

Williams's two daughters. Growing up in Compton, California, Serena excelled in tennis from an early age, motivated in part by her desire to compete with her older sister, Venus.

As you probably know, Serena and Venus both became elite players, unquestionably two of the best that the sport of tennis has ever seen. They have each been ranked number one in the world during their careers. Serena turned pro in 1995 and won the US Open in 1999, her first major championship, beating Martina Hingis 6–3, 7–6 in the finals. In 2003, Serena completed a Career Grand Slam—that is, winning all four of the major tournaments.

Along with their individual accomplishments, by 2015 the Williams sisters had won 21 doubles titles playing together, including 13 Grand Slam titles and three Olympic gold medals. They have faced off against each other in a total of eight Grand Slam individual tournament finals. Serena holds the edge with a record of 6–2.

Richard wanted his daughters to learn the game on the public tennis courts in Compton to gain an appreciation of the importance of hard work and getting an education. Compton, located south of downtown Los Angeles, is notorious for high crime rates. There were holes in the nets, and the Williamses had to sweep glass off the courts. "If you can keep playing tennis when somebody is shooting a gun down the street, that's concentration," Serena later said.

In 1988, Richard was ready to pass the coaching reins to a professional tennis instructor. He reached out to Paul Cohen, who had taught many of the top players in the game, including John McEnroe, Pete Sampras, Michael Chang, Vitas Gerulaitis, and Stan Smith. Richard brought his daughters to Brentwood, California, and Cohen began to coach them. Under Cohen's tutelage, the girls began to shine.

In 1991, Richard was ready to take the next step. He contacted Florida pro tennis coach Rick Macci. Macci was coaching tennis prodigy Jennifer Capriati, who had made her professional debut in 1990 at the age of 13. At the 1992 Barcelona Olympics, Capriati came from a set down in the finals to defeat top-seeded Steffi Graf to capture the gold medal. She was only 16 years old.

Macci was impressed with the Williams sisters when he visited them in May 1991. In September of that year, the entire Williams family moved to Delray Beach, Florida, and the girls enrolled in the Rick Macci Tennis Academy. In addition to tennis, their training regimen included tae kwon do, gymnastics, boxing, and ballet. Cohen continued to train the sisters during their return visits to California.

Venus turned pro at age 14, on October 31, 1994. In the first round of the Bank of the West Classic in Oakland, California, she shocked 58th-ranked Shaun Stafford in straight sets, 6–3, 6–4. In the second round, Venus won the first set against world No. 1 Arantxa Sanchez-Vicario, before losing in three sets. In 1995, Reebok signed Venus to a 5-year endorsement deal worth $12 million.

In October 1995, Serena turned pro at age 14. Her debut wasn't as auspicious as her sister's. She was bounced in the qualifying round of the Bell Challenge in Quebec by seventh-seeded Anne Miller, 6–1, 6–1. The match lasted less than an hour and left a bitter taste in Serena's mouth. "I didn't play like I meant to play. I played kind of like an amateur," she said afterward. However, this did not deter Serena at all, and she refocused on her training with a champion's mind-set.

Serena did not play a tournament in 1996, but she continued to work hard on her game. In November 1997, Serena, ranked No. 304 in the world, entered the Ameritech Cup in Chicago. She upset both No. 7 Mary Pierce and No. 4 Monica Seles before succumbing in the semifinals to No. 5 Lindsay Davenport. Serena ended the year with a world No. 99 ranking. Armed with a powerful serve, a strong mind, and a competitive spirit, she was rapidly coming into her own.

In February 1999, Serena won her first professional singles title when she defeated No. 18 Amélie Mauresmo at the Open Gaz de France finals, 6–2, 3–6, 7–6. Only 3 years later, on July 8, 2002, Serena reached No. 1 in the world. More recently, in 2015, Serena, who is now one of the older players on the tour, won her sixth Austrian Open. In June of that year, she won her third French Open title by overcoming the flu and Lucie Safarova to carry the day 6–3, 6–7, 6–2. The following month, she claimed her sixth Wimbledon win for her 21st career major title.

Here are the strategies Serena utilizes, organized according to the Champion's Comeback Code.

- **LET GO:** To release mental bricks, Serena keeps moving forward. She explained how she handles tough defeats: "I decided I can't pay a person to rewind time, so I may as well get over it." Serena's sole focus is always on this point, this set, this match, and this tournament, because the present moment is the only time to make great things happen. In her life, she strives to balance tennis with her many other interests, including acting and fashion. But she always keeps tournament play her top priority.

- **LOOK FOR SUPPORT:** Serena's sister, Venus, is her best friend, greatest supporter, and toughest opponent. Her family and friends keep her grounded. And she constantly thanks all of her fans for their support. "Family's first, and that's what matters most. We realize that our love goes deeper than the tennis game," Serena said.

• **LOVE THE GAME:** Serena has always played the game with purpose and passion. "What's going to make me happy is going on the court and holding up trophies, singles and doubles," she said. Serena loves the opportunity to compete and always plays to win.

• **LEARN:** Serena has embraced a growth mind-set throughout her illustrious career, as evidenced by her continual study of the techniques and tactics of the game. At the 2012 French Open, Serena was upset in the first round. Afterward, she teamed up with tennis coach Patrick Mouratoglou, who helped her return to her winning ways. "I'm pretty much insatiable. I feel there's so many things I can improve on," she said.

• **LABOR:** Known as one of the most industrious players on the WTA Tour, Serena inherited her incredible work ethic from her father, who told her and Venus that dreams are the only things that come to a sleeper, but that dreams come true if you work hard. Regarding her success, Serena said, "Luck has nothing to do with [my success], because I have spent many, many hours, countless hours, on the court working for my one moment in time, not knowing when it would come."

• **LEARN OPTIMISM:** Serena believes in herself, especially while battling injuries and during performance slumps. "I've had to learn to fight all my life—got to learn to keep smiling. If you smile, things will work out." In fact, Serena has said that losing only makes her more motivated.

• **LEAN ON YOUR MENTAL GAME:** In tennis, victory often comes to those who want it the most. Serena persistently shows her opponents that she wants to win more than they do. Even when she's not at her best, she digs deep and bounces back. "I've always considered myself the best and the top. I never considered that I was out of it," Serena said.

In the 2012 US Open final against Victoria Azarenka, Serena was down 3–5 in the third set before winning four consecutive games to prevail 6–2, 2–6, 7–5. At Wimbledon in 2015, Serena bounced back from a set down, doing this for an amazing 34th time during a Grand Slam in her career. How does she bring the best out of herself when she needs to the most? Positive self-talk. "When I'm down, I talk to myself a lot. I look crazy because I'm constantly having an argument with myself," she said. The argument is between her Good Wolf and her Bad Wolf. The Good Wolf usually wins.

To be a champion in your own game and life, you have to find the willingness to hang tough in the face of impossible odds, whether in a competition or some other obstacle life throws at you. In making a comeback, almost everyone will tell you that you face insurmountable odds. Overcoming such obstacles is what makes us champions. There is no doubt that Serena Williams, along with her sister and father, overcame many obstacles. Not only did they take on these challenges, they did so with positivity, enthusiasm, and infinite self-confidence.

THE FINAL TAKEAWAY

You can reach your full potential, transform minor setbacks into major comebacks, and refuse to back down when victory seems out of reach. Like Tom Izzo, Ben Hogan, and Serena Williams, you can apply and join the 300 Club. You are now armed and ready to write your own comeback story!

EPILOGUE

WHAT IS YOUR COMEBACK STORY?

If a story is in you, it has to come out.

—WILLIAM FAULKNER

The New England Patriots and the Seattle Seahawks made impressive comebacks throughout the 2014 NFL regular season and playoffs. The Patriots had a slow start to the season, capped by a crushing 41–14 loss to the Kansas City Chiefs in week 4 to drop them to a 2–2 record. They rebounded to finish the season 12–4, however, winning their sixth straight AFC East title. In the AFC Divisional Playoffs, they rallied from two different 14-point deficits to knock off the Baltimore Ravens 35–31. In the AFC Championship, they crushed the Indianapolis Colts 45–7 to earn a trip to the Super Bowl.

Meanwhile, the Seahawks limped along to a 3–3 start to the season. They then went on a 9–1 tear to finish 12–4 and repeat as NFC West champions. In the NFC Divisional Playoffs, they bounced the Carolina Panthers 31–17. In the NFC Championship game, the Seahawks fell behind 16–0 in the third quarter to the Green Bay Packers. They had closed the gap to 19–14 with 2:09 left in regulation. The Seahawks recovered an onside kick and quickly scored to take a 22–19 lead. The Packers tied the game with a 48-yard field goal as time expired. In overtime, the Seahawks drove 87 yards to win the game 28–22. The defending Super Bowl champions were back.

On February 1, 2015, the Patriots and Seahawks faced off in Super Bowl XLIX. The game was tied at 14 at halftime, but the Seahawks grabbed a 10-point lead heading into the fourth quarter. The Patriots, however, made their own run to take a 28–24 lead with only 2 minutes remaining. The Seahawks made a last-ditch effort to win the game. They drove all the way down the field, but undrafted cornerback Malcolm Butler's goal-line interception with 20 seconds left clinched the Patriots' Super Bowl title. Patriots quarterback Tom Brady was named the game's Most Valuable Player.

After the dramatic win, Patriots owner Robert Kraft talked about the team's "mental toughness." Mental toughness had been the team's mantra all season. "It was a lot of mental toughness," said Tom Brady after winning his fourth Super Bowl. "Our team has had it all year. We never doubted each other, so that's what it took." During the season, Brady was heavily criticized by the media, especially after the Patriots were drubbed by the Chiefs. "Every team has a journey," said Brady, "and a lot of people lost faith in us . . . but we held strong, we held together, and it's a great feeling."

The Seahawks were understandably devastated. But they had the guts to put it all on the line and really go for it all season long. They came within inches of winning back-to-back Super Bowl titles. Ever the optimist, coach Pete Carroll took to Twitter the next day: "This is really hard to take now but in the long run it will make us stronger. Our guys are so strong and our future is bright." Champions recover, reflect, and reignite. Anything else is a waste of time.

Champions don't dwell on their defeats by playing the "What if?" game. After all, they did what they set out to do, which was to do the best they could do. They didn't beat themselves. To move forward, they celebrate what they want to see happen more often, learn the lessons that need to be learned, and then dump out the rest. Defeats and disappointments are an integral part of sports and life; it's how well you respond to these setbacks that makes you a true champion.

Since turning pro in 2002 at the age of 17, Swiss tennis player Stan Wawrinka has dealt with defeats and disappointments. In 2007, he tore a tendon in his right knee and was sidelined for 3 months. He has had to spend a lot of time in the shadow of fellow countryman and all-time great Roger Federer. In 2008, however, they teamed up as doubles partners and won gold at the 2008 Beijing Olympics. Until 2010, Wawrinka's sole ATP title was at the 2006 Croatia Open Umag. His opponent in the final, Novak Djokovic, had to resign because of breathing difficulties during the tiebreak of the first set.

In recent years, Wawrinka, who is armed with a one-handed backhand that is a thing of beauty, a lightning-fast serve, and a much-improved forehand, has not required opponent forfeits to earn his way to the top of the podium. At the 2014 Australian Open, he beat world No. 1 Rafael Nadal in the final, his first win over Nadal in 13 attempts! Then, in 2015, he won his second Grand Slam at the French Open, coming from behind to beat top-seeded Novak Djokovic in the final. He now has 10 career titles—and counting. At the age of 30, an elder statesman in tennis and sports, he's playing his best ever.

Wawrinka has a tattoo on his left forearm that quotes the Irish playwright Samuel Beckett: "Ever tried. Ever failed. No matter.

Try again. Fail again. Fail better." Beckett's words have guided Wawrinka's career. They give him the courage to continue and the motivation to improve. He tried, failed, and tried again until he finally succeeded. No matter.

What can we learn from Wawrinka and other champions that took the long road? First, don't give up—*step up*! Use the 7 L's to crack the Champion's Comeback Code. Here are bounce-back affirmations to help you write your own comeback story,

1. I *let go* of and leave behind all mental bricks from mistakes or defeats, or I build a champion's castle with them.

2. I *look for support* and build a winning team around me. Negativity from others is used as motivational fuel to elevate my performance.

3. I *love the game* by competing with purpose and passion.

4. I *learn* by embracing a growth mind-set. I'm not afraid of "losing" because I know that losing means learning.

5. I *labor* by pounding the rock through hard and intelligent work in practice and training.

6. I *learn optimism* by believing in my comeback story. It is my story, and I'm the author.

7. I *lean on my mental game* because I sharpen my mental skills to a razor's edge through regular practice.

We play sports for the stories, some good, some bad. There is no greater motivation than wanting to tell a good story. You are now ready to take the first step on your next journey. Think about the comeback story you want to tell for the rest of your life. Then write it.

But perhaps you are wondering how long your comeback will take?

Consider this story: A climber is about to hike up the steep path of a tall mountain. The climber sees a wise old man sitting on a rock near the base of the mountain playing a flute. The climber interrupts the man's playing with the following question: "Could you please tell me how long it will take to reach the summit?" The old man responds, "Walk!"

The climber is confused and repeats the question, only to receive the same answer. He shakes his head and continues toward the summit. After a while, he suddenly hears the voice of the old man from down below. The old man shouts, "Seven hours!" He could only now answer the question, since he had not previously seen how fast the climber was walking.

So start walking, and best wishes on writing your own comeback story!

ACKNOWLEDGMENTS

Many thanks to my champion literary agent Helen Zimmermann for her excellent guidance and support. The second time is better still.

Much appreciation to Ursula Cary Ziemba, my editor, for her clarity and direction. I'd also like to thank Mark Weinstein, Evan Klonsky, Susan Turner, Amy King, Nancy Bailey, Isabelle Hughes, and the rest of the world-class team at Rodale Books.

Thanks to Chrissy Barth, Kim Chronister, , Zach Davis, Tim DiFrancesco, James FitzGerald, Tanner Gers, Margaret Hoelzer, Jake Mace, Gloria Petruzzelli, and Bryon Powell for their excellent contributions.

Special thanks to my wonderful wife, Anne, and our darling daughter, Maria Paz, for their love and encouragement.

REFERENCES AND
RECOMMENDED READING

Abel, E. L., and M. L. Kruger. "Smile Intensity in Photographs Predicts Longevity." *Psychological Science* 21, no. 4 (February 2010): 542–4.

Affleck, Glenn, Howard Tennen, and Andrea Apter. "Optimism, Pessimism, and Daily Life with Chronic Illness." In *Optimism and Pessimism: Implications for Theory, Research, and Practice*, edited by Edward C. Chang, 147–68. Washington, DC: American Psychological Association, 2001.

Afremow, Jim. *The Champion's Mind: How Great Athletes Think, Train, and Thrive*. New York: Rodale, 2014.

Alarcon, Gene M., Nathan A. Bowling, and Steven Khazon. "Great Expectations: A Meta-Analytic Examination of Optimism and Hope." *Personality and Individual Differences* 54, no. 7 (May 2013): 821–27.

Auriemma, Geno, with Jackie MacMullan. *Geno: In Pursuit of Perfection*. New York: Grand Central Publishing, 2009.

———. *The Psychology behind Fitness Motivation: A Revolutionary New Program to Lose Weight and Stay Fit for Life*. CreateSpace (self-published), 2013.

Chronister, Kim. *FitMentality: The Ultimate Guide to Stop Binge Eating*. CreateSpace (self-published), 2015.

Davis, Zach. *Appalachian Trials: A Psychological and Emotional Guide to Successfully Thru-Hiking the Appalachian Trail*. Good Badger Publishing (self-published), 2012.

Dolcos, Sanda, and Dolores Albarracin. "The Inner Speech of Behavioral Regulation: Intentions and Task Performance Strengthen When You Talk to Yourself as a You." *European Journal of Social Psychology* 44, no. 6 (October 2014): 636–42.

Dweck, Carol S. *Mindset: The New Psychology of Success*. New York: Random House, 2007.

Kabat-Zinn, John. *Wherever You Go, There You Are: Mindfulness Meditation in Everyday Life*. New York: Hyperion, 2005.

Lazenby, Roland. *Michael Jordan: The Life*. New York: Little, Brown and Company, 2014.

Miller, Frank, and Lynn Varley. *300*. Dark Horse Books, 1999.

Millman, Dan. *Way of the Peaceful Warrior: A Book That Changes Lives*. Revised ed. Tiburon, CA: HJ Kramer, 2006.

Moore, Richard. *Slaying the Badger: Greg LeMond, Bernard Hinault, and the Greatest Tour de France*. Boulder, CO: Velo Press, 2012.

Nyad, Diana. *Find a Way*. New York: Alfred A. Knopf, 2015.

Peterson, Christopher, and Lisa M. Bossio, Lisa. "Optimism and Physical Well-Being." In *Optimism and Pessimism: Implications for Theory, Research, and Practice*, edited by Edward C. Chang, 127–45. Washington, DC: American Psychological Association, 2001.

Peterson, Christopher, Nansook Park, and Eric S. Kim. "Can Optimism Decrease the Risk of Illness and Disease Among the Elderly?" *Aging Health* 8, no. 1 (2012): 5–8.

Powell, Bryon. *Relentless Forward Progress: A Guide to Running Ultramarathons*. Halcottsville, NY: Breakaway Books, 2011.

Rotella, Bob, with Bob Cullen. *Golf Is Not a Game of Perfect*. New York: Simon & Schuster, 1995.

Sampson, Curt. *Hogan*. Updated ed. Nashville, TN: Thomas Nelson, 2001.

Scheier, Michael F., and Charles S. Carver. "Effects of Optimism on Psychological and Physical Well-Being: Theoretical Overview and Empirical Update." *Cognitive Therapy and Research* 16, no. 2 (1992): 201–28.

Scheier, Michael F.; Charles S. Carver, and Michael W. Bridges. "Optimism, Pessimism, and Psychological Well-Being." In *Optimism and Pessimism: Implications for Theory, Research, and Practice*, edited by Edward C. Chang, 189–216. Washington, DC: American Psychological Association, 2001.

Seligman, Martin E. P. *Learned Optimism: How to Change Your Mind and Your Life*. Reprint ed. New York: Vintage, 2006.

St-Pierre, Georges, with Justin Kingsley. *The Way of the Fight*. New York: William Morrow, 2013,

Wellington, Chrissie. *A Life without Limits: A World Champion's Journey*. New York: Center Street, 2012.

Williams, Serena, with Daniel Paisner. *On the Line*. New York: Grand Central Publishing, 2009.

INDEX

ABOUT THE AUTHOR

Dr. Jim Afremow is a much sought-after mental game coach, licensed professional counselor, and the author of *The Champion's Mind: How Great Athletes Think, Train, and Thrive.* He is the founder of Good to Gold Medal, PLLC, a leading coaching and consulting practice located in Phoenix, Arizona. Dr. Afremow provides individual and team mental training services across the globe to athletes, teams, and coaches in all sports, as well as to parents, business professionals, and others engaged in highly demanding endeavors. He is passionate about helping others achieve peak performance and personal excellence to reach their true potential.

For more than 15 years, Dr. Afremow has assisted numerous recreational, high school, collegiate, and professional athletes. He has worked with athletes from all several major leagues, including MLB, NBA, WNBA, PGA Tour, LPGA Tour, NHL, and NFL. In addition, he has mentally trained several U.S. and international Olympic competitors. He served as the staff mental coach for two international Olympic teams—the Greek Olympic softball team and India's Olympic field hockey team. From 2004 to 2013, he served as the sports psychology specialist with Counseling Services and Sports Medicine at Arizona State University.

Dr. Afremow is a member of the Association for Applied Sport

Psychology, the American Counseling Association, and the Arizona Psychoanalytic Society. He has an extensive history of professional activity, including conducting conference presentations and corporate workshops, and he has published in top journals and peer-reviewed publications, including the *Journal of Sport and Exercise Psychology* and *Olympic Coach* magazine. He has also served as an expert blogger on the mental side of athletics for *Psychology Today* and the *Sporting News*.

Dr. Afremow resides in Phoenix, Arizona, with his wife, Anne, and their daughter, Maria Paz.